PORK
CHOP

PORK CHOP

60 RECIPES FOR LIVING HIGH ON THE HOG

RAY "DR. BBQ" LAMPE

Photographs by Jody Horton

CHRONICLE BOOKS

SAN FRANCISCO

Library of Congress Cataloging-in-Publication Data available.

ISBN 978-1-4521-1367-8

Manufactured in China

Designed by **Vanessa Dina**

Prop and food styling by **Kate LeSueur**

Cooking by **Angela Howe**

Typesetting by **DC Type**

For more information about pork, visit **PorkBeInspired.com**

10 9 8 7 6 5 4 3 2 1

Chronicle Books LLC
680 Second Street
San Francisco, California 94107
www.chroniclebooks.com

This book is dedicated to all the hardworking American pork producers. Our meat cases are full of perfect pork because of you. Thanks!

Acknowledgments

I'd like to thank all the good folks from the American pork industry for creating such a wonderful product to work with. Thanks to Sandi for putting up with me and tasting all those pork chops. Thanks to Bill LeBlond, Amy Treadwell, Doug Ogan, Marie Oishi, Vanessa Dina, Tera Killip, Peter Perez, and David Hawk at Chronicle Books for keeping me around and making me look so good. Thanks to Scott Mendel for always finding a way to make things work. Last, but not least, thanks to Traci Rodemeyer for all the help and friendship.

FOREWORD

Overstatement among food writers is so prevalent, it's like a tsunami from an earthquake hitting during a hurricane. So let me meekly declare that the pork chop is the finest cut of meat any human could ever hope to eat. It also happens to feed our most primal urge.

Before man learned to walk upright and make reservations on his phone for a table for two at the place where cooks make pea-size food using liquid nitrogen, he roamed the earth in search of meaty goodness to eat with the teeth that nature put at his disposal. Being smaller than a cow, slower than a rabbit, nicer than a bear, and meatier than a bird, pigs made for a dandy meal.

Once caught, there were many parts of the animal one could consume. My guess is that the process of elimination led the species *Homo sapiens* to follow its taste buds to the most flavorful options between the parenthetical snout and tail. Add some fire to the process and you can see why the pork chop would stand out immediately to our ancestor.

First of all, with its T-shaped bone, the chop comes with its own handle. This is no small thing. Just as with their very good friends, the teeth, opposable thumbs were created for using. Food that came with a built-in place to grab made eating dinner easier while running from things that wanted to eat us as well. It's the circle of life. It flows through us all.

Yes, the ribs are delicious. But you have to eat a hundred of them to make a meal (not that there is anything wrong with that). Indeed, the leg offers a handle, but there are only four of those per pig and only two of them are tasty. The belly is the tempting candy jar of the animal, but you can only eat so much of that before the pigs start looking at you like dinner. Primitive man may have been primitive, but he found the tender part of the porker in the chop region and made it work for him.

I learned to cook pork chops by watching my father. I was lucky enough to grow up at a time when gas grills were starting to be affordable. My dad, who did not make an enormous sum of money as a car salesman, nonetheless installed a Charmglow grill in the backyard in the early 1970s. Because this was the Stone Age of grilling, back when an ankle-high hibachi or a campfire was the most you could hope for, he built a concrete platform for it and bolted the grill down, weather be damned. A grill with wheels might as well have been from *The Jetsons*.

My dad fine-tuned his grilling expertise over the years until he finally figured out the precise combination of tenderizing marinade, spice, and heat to apply for the best results. Steak was an occasional luxury and fish hit our plate only when it hit the bait on his hook. Chicken parts always made the fire flare and my father curse. For the family of a guy selling Chevrolets and Buicks, pork was the affordable—and delicious—option while he learned how to get the most out of the family grill.

I grew up in the same city where Ray Lampe now lives. That Ray and I just so happen to live in the exact part of the world where the pig first came ashore in the Americas is no happy accident. Pork is a magnet that attracts all men.

But make no mistake: Geography has nothing to do with Ray's expertise. Across this delicious nation and around the world, he has honed his skills at cook-offs, throwdowns, and smokefests at a champion level that approaches ninja status. Simply put, Ray is a global master of the pig.

In this book, you will find—as I did—that there are more ways to enhance your chop-eating enjoyment than you ever thought possible. Ray's sense for making pork even more delicious than it comes in its original packaging is calibrated more acutely than that of mortal cooks. In his hands you can feel secure that not only are you making the tastiest and most tender cut of the pig, you're doing so in the company of an expert.

He is, after all, a doctor of barbecue.

Jeff Houck
The Tampa Tribune

INTRODUCTION

THE WORLD IS MY PORK CHOP

I once had a bumper sticker that read "The World Is My Pork Chop." Needless to say, I made a lot of new friends because of it. Maybe I'm a little over the top, but I believe we all have a love affair with pork chops. They may not be the high-end meal at great steak houses, but they're always on the menu. And on those pricey menus, pork chops are the best value, and they're delicious! When Mrs. Cunningham wanted to butter up Howard on the classic sitcom *Happy Days*, she served him pork chops. In Mayberry, Andy's favorite meal from Aunt Bee's kitchen was pork chops. The dish that started the "on-a-stick" craze at state fairs was the pork chop on a stick. I could go on.

Pork chops are just about everyone's favorite cut from the beloved pig. They come from the loin area up on top of the pig. That's the part we're talking about when we refer to something good as being "high on the hog." Pork chops are lean enough to be healthful, but flavorful enough to stand up to a wide variety of preparations, both in the kitchen and on the outdoor grill. And while we all love to cook and eat pork chops, we've only just scratched the surface of their culinary potential. I love pork chops grilled or breaded and fried. But I also love them on a Philly-style sandwich with cheese and onions, or with Spanish rice in a dish I call Arroz con Puerco Chops (page 91). They're savory-delicious when cooked long and slow with white beans or jerk-style

on the grill. But we're not done there. Pork chops are low enough in fat to top a chopped salad or jump in a wrap with spinach and feta cheese. I like them on flat bread, in stir-fry, as Buffalo Hot Chop Sandwiches (page 113), Pork Chops Parmigiana (page 102), and even Pork Chop–Stuffed French Toast (page 109). They're all here for you to enjoy and all written with my own spin after forty years in the kitchen. I'm known as "Dr. BBQ" and I'm proud to wear that moniker. Grilling and smoking are a passion for me and I love to cook that way, but I've spent a lot of time at the range as well. Even *I* don't light the charcoal every day. While pork chops are wonderful grilled, they lend themselves beautifully to so many other great preparations. And with a couple of quick knife cuts that any home cook should be comfortable with, the possibilities are endless.

The recipes in this book are here to help you enjoy pork chops in some new and tasty ways. But like any recipe or cookbook that I write, I encourage you to tweak things to the tastes that you and your guests prefer. Don't let an ingredient that you don't care for keep you from making a recipe that, otherwise, sounds good. Make it your own! Adjust the recipes to fit the tastes of your guests and enjoy.

In a Homer Simpson kind of way, I've spent a lot of time dreaming about pork chops and how to use them in all of my favorite dishes. Now I get to share them with you, and the results are going to make a lot of pork chop fans very happy.

Pork chops come from the top of the hog in the loin area, and because of that they're all fairly lean, healthful, tender, and easy to cook. And when cooked properly, pork chops are extremely succulent. The loin of a typical hog is about 18 in/46 cm long, and the cuts vary quite a bit from front to back. In general, the chops from the front of the hog are smaller and well marbled, getting leaner and larger as they head farther back. But in this case, leaner doesn't mean less flavor. Some may even argue that the lean sirloin chops taste better, with their deep porky flavor and dense texture. The flavor will vary with the thickness of the cut as well. Thick chops are often eaten medium-rare for a juicy, rich, steak-like flavor, while thin chops are typically cooked through, with a firm texture that remains tender just because of the cut. To me, they're kind of like children. I love them all in their own way. And while they are mostly inter-changeable, the better we know these cuts, the better we can choose and cook them properly.

TYPES OF PORK CHOPS

Starting toward the front of the hog, we have the BLADE CHOPS. These are cut from the beginning of the loin in the shoulder area. They may contain some blade bone as well as back-rib bone. Blade chops are usually cut thicker and are well marbled. These are often butterflied and sold as pork loin country-style ribs. These are well suited to roasting and slow grilling.

Next up are RIBEYE CHOPS. These originate in the center of the loin in the rib area and may include some back and rib bone. In general, rib chops are the most tender of all pork chops, with the heaviest marbling, and I believe they are the best choice for hot grilling.

Behind the ribeye chops are the PORTERHOUSE CHOPS. They have that characteristic T-bone shape and are very popular in restaurants because of the look. These chops include a lot of top loin meat as well as a bit of tenderloin meat. They're called porterhouse chops because of their regal appearance and are well suited to grilling and frying.

Behind the ribeye chops is also the area where we get the NEW YORK CHOP, also known as the boneless top loin chop. This is a boneless chop cut from the top loin muscle and is what I think of when I hear the term "The Other White Meat." These lean chops are the most versatile and, while they're great on the grill when cut 1 in/2.5 cm thick or more, they can be cut thinner too for what I call "breakfast" chops, or easily cut into smaller pieces for use in sandwiches, stews, and casseroles.

Last but not least, bringing up the rear are SIRLOIN CHOPS. These are cut from the hip area and sometimes include part of the hip bone. They lack a bit in their marbling, but when cooked properly represent a great value with a very meaty pork flavor.

BLADE CHOPS

RIBEYE CHOPS

PORTERHOUSE CHOPS

NEW YORK CHOPS

SIRLOIN CHOPS

Quality

While pork isn't graded by the United States Department of Agriculture (USDA) as is beef, that doesn't mean there aren't different levels of quality available. Most of us choose our pork from the case at the grocery store or warehouse club, and that's not a bad idea at all. Fresh American pork is a wonderfully consistent product with solid nutritional value and great taste and tenderness. America's pork producers have worked together to create a very good supply of pork for Americans to enjoy, keeping the prices in line and the quality top notch. But these days, there are other options, and some of them are quite tasty. Breed-specific pork has gotten a lot of buzz in the food world, and rightfully so. Farmers have always chosen the breed of hog that best fits their climate, available food sources, and customer preference. But now some are promoting their breed of choice as a way to set themselves apart. Chefs and retailers do a lot of research to find out what consumers want, and sometimes you just want something a little different. That's where the less-common breeds excel and appeal to different palates. These breeds are often referred to as "heirloom" or "heritage" breeds. Examples in the marketplace today include Berkshire (also known as Kurobuta, meaning "black pig"), Duroc, and Tamworth. Some or all of these may be available near you, but in other areas would be very hard to find. My best advice is to see what's available in your market. Try asking your local butcher or the high-end fresh grocery store if they have any heirloom pork or if they know where you might find some. Try the local farmers' market, too. Or track down a local chef with a local cuisine reputation. Only after you find what's available can you decide if the price and quality meet your wants and needs.

Shopping

Always look for fresh packaging and red color. Raw pork should not be pale or white in color. A thin ribbon of fat along the outside is a good thing and little flecks of fat throughout the meat (also known as marbling) are an even better thing. Choose the chops that look good to you. In the recipes throughout this book, I always call for bone-in or boneless pork chops and occasionally a specific cut like the porterhouse chop. Feel free to substitute the cuts that you like and what looks good in the meat case that day, and if there is a specific cut on sale that week and it looks good, go for it. My only rule would be to try to use the same thickness called for in the recipe or you'll have to adjust the cooking times.

You'll find packaging claims on fresh pork that suggest the product inside is special in some way. Here are some of the buzzwords that will help you understand what you're getting into when you go shopping for pork. Once again, you'll need to find what's available in your area and then decide if the price and quality meet your wants and needs.

LOCALLY GROWN One of the more easily understood terms, although without USDA guidelines attached. This really indicates more of an economic decision based on the consumer wanting to support local farmers. The definition of "local" can vary, depending mainly on what is available to you.

FREE RANGE Also referred to as "pasture-raised," "free-roaming," and "raised outdoors." The USDA standard to make this claim for pork is that hogs have had continuous access to pasture for at least 80 percent of their production cycle.

NO ANTIBIOTICS "No antibiotics added" on the label means that the hogs were raised without using antibiotics and that documentation has been provided to the USDA demonstrating this.

NATURAL Pork products that are in compliance with the USDA Natural Standards mean the products contain no artificial ingredients or added color and are only minimally processed. The label must explain the use of the term "natural" (such as no added colorings or artificial ingredients; minimally processed).

NATURALLY RAISED There is currently no USDA standard for making a "naturally raised" claim on pork products. That means that the definition could vary from one pork product to another, rendering the term pretty much useless. It could mean that the hog was raised without antibiotics or animal by-products in the feed. It could also indicate the use of deep straw bedding, or that the hog was raised outdoors, etc. Any of these attributes will likely be stated on the packaging.

ORGANIC This specifies an entire process in which synthetic inputs into all phases of animal production, meat processing, and handling are prohibited. Labeling rules have been established by the USDA for products claiming to be organic and include four categories:

100% Organic—Products produced exclusively using organic methods as defined by the USDA. This pork can carry the USDA organic certification seal.

Organic—95 percent or greater of the ingredients are organically produced with the remaining 5 percent of the ingredients on the National List of Allowed Synthetic and Prohibited Non-Synthetic Substances. This pork can also carry the USDA organic certification seal.

Made with Organic—70 to 95 percent of the ingredients are organically produced and should be displayed on the principal display panel as "Made with organic [specific ingredient(s)]."

Less than 70 percent Organic—These products have the option to include "X percent organic" on the information panel and only need to list organic ingredients on the ingredient statement.

THE ESSENTIALS OF PORK CHOP COOKERY

DONENESS

The single most important factor in serving tender and juicy pork chops is getting them cooked to the proper degree of doneness. Pork chops can be made tender and delicious in many ways. The simplest ways are grilling, broiling, and panfrying, and when you're using these methods, it's important to know that pork chops are safely cooked at an internal temperature of 145°F/60°C, followed by a 3-minute rest time. Cooking to that temperature makes for a pink, juicy, and delicious chop that we all know is safe to eat. Most Americans now enjoy eating their pork chops pink and juicy, and cooks are very happy about that. But just like any other cut, some people don't like their meat pink, so as it cooks it's our job to please our guests. I will cook the chops a little more if asked. But please don't go over 155°F/70°C. Below that should get rid of the pink but still yield a juicy and tender pork chop. Any temperature above that can make for a tough and dry piece of pork, and I don't recommend it.

If you're going to cook your chops using a long slow-cooked method, the rules are a little different. Pork chops are versatile and do very well in soups, stews, and braised dishes, where we cook them well beyond the pink and juicy state. I don't use my temperature gauge for these dishes and rely mainly on the touch-and-feel method. When the chops feel tender to my fingers, they are done.

BASIC PORK CHOP COOKING TIMES

Each recipe has directions for proper doneness, but here is a chart that
gives you general guidelines for cooking pork chops.

GRILLING OVER DIRECT, MEDIUM HEAT

Turn once halfway through cooking

Loin Chops, Bone-In or Boneless ¾ in/2 cm thick	145°F/60°C	8 to 10 minutes total time
Loin Chops, Bone-In or Boneless 1 in/2.5 cm thick	145°F/60°C	10 to 12 minutes total time
Loin Chops, Bone-In or Boneless 1½ in/4 cm thick	145°F/60°C	12 to 14 minutes total time

BROILING 4 TO 5 IN/10 TO 12 CM FROM HEAT

Turn once halfway through cooking

Loin Chops, Bone-In or Boneless ¾ in/2 cm thick	145°F/60°C	8 to 10 minutes total time
Loin Chops, Bone-In or Boneless 1 in/2.5 cm thick	145°F/60°C	10 to 12 minutes total time
Loin Chops, Bone-In or Boneless 1½ in/4 cm thick	145°F/60°C	12 to 14 minutes total time

SAUTÉING

Loin Chops, Bone-In or Boneless ¾ in/2 cm thick	145°F/60°C	8 to 10 minutes total time
Loin Chops, Bone-In or Boneless 1 in/2.5 cm thick	145°F/60°C	10 to 12 minutes total time
Loin Chops, Bone-In or Boneless 1½ in/4 cm thick	145°F/60°C	12 to 14 minutes total time

BRAISING OR STEWING

Loin Chops, Bone-In or Boneless ¾ in/2 cm thick	30 to 40 minutes total time until tender
Loin Chops, Bone-In or Boneless 1 in/2.5 cm thick	40 to 50 minutes total time until tender
Loin Chops, Bone-In or Boneless 1½ in/4 cm thick	50 to 60 minutes total time until tender

SPICING

The recipes in this book all include the proper seasonings, and you'll see a trend. Salt, pepper, and granulated garlic are naturals with pork chops. Onion powder, chili powder, and a bit of sugar all go well too, and you'll see them show up often, along with paprika. Paprika in small amounts doesn't have much flavor, but I often use it to season my pork chops to encourage browning without overcooking.

Following are a couple of all-purpose pork chop spice blends that you might enjoy. The first is an all-purpose seasoned salt and the second is a grilling rub that works well on pork chops and just about anything else. They both store well, so make a batch and keep them around the kitchen.

Pork Chop Seasoned Salt

¼ cup/75 g salt

1 tbsp sugar

1 tsp granulated garlic

1 tsp granulated onion

1 tsp paprika

¼ tsp ground turmeric

¼ tsp ground thyme

In a small bowl, combine the ingredients and mix well. Store the mix in an airtight container for up to 6 months.

Makes about ⅜ cup/95 g

Dr. BBQ's Pork Chop Grill Rub

¼ cup/60 g Sugar In The Raw

3 tbsp salt

2 tbsp paprika

2 tbsp chili powder

1 tbsp granulated garlic

1 tsp granulated onion

1 tsp black pepper

¼ tsp cayenne pepper

¼ tsp ground allspice

In a small bowl, combine the ingredients and mix well. Store the rub in an airtight container for up to 6 months.

Makes about ¾ cup/90 g

Pork Stock

You won't typically find pork broth or pork stock at the grocery store and, frankly, I'm not sure why. You will find vegetable stock and that's what I normally use with pork. Occasionally a recipe will benefit from the flavor of chicken or beef stock or even a combination of the two. But if you really want to kick up the porky flavor in your dishes, you can make pork stock. It's not hard; it just requires some pork bones and spending the day close to the kitchen. Like any other stock, this freezes well, so doing it once can make for a nice stash of porky goodness that will last for months.

5 lb/2.3 kg pork neck bones

1 lb/455 g pork scraps (if available)

Salt

Black pepper

2 onions, quartered

3 carrots, peeled and cut into 3-in/7.5-cm pieces

2 celery stalks, cut into 3-in/7.5-cm pieces

4 or 5 sprigs fresh thyme

1 tbsp tomato paste

1 bay leaf

1 tsp whole black peppercorns

Preheat the oven to 425°F/220°C. Spread the neck bones and pork scraps (if using) on a large baking sheet. Season them with salt and pepper. Roast for 1 hour, until the bones are golden brown. Transfer the bones and pork scraps to a heavy stockpot of at least 8 qt/7.5 L. Add the onions, carrots, celery, thyme, tomato paste, bay leaf, peppercorns, and ½ tsp salt. Work the vegetables down into the bones. Add 3 qt/3 L water just to cover everything. Place the pot over medium heat and cover. Bring it to a low simmer. Reduce the temperature to maintain a low simmer. Cook for 3 to 4 hours, until the meat falls from the bones. Remove the pot from the heat and let it rest for 30 minutes. With a slotted spoon, remove the bones, meat, and vegetables. Strain the stock through a sieve, then a second time through a fine-mesh sieve or a sieve lined with cheesecloth. Discard the solids. Refrigerate the stock until cold, at least 4 hours and preferably overnight. Remove the fat from the top before using.

Makes about 2 qt/2 L

TOOLS OF THE TRADE

These are the things that I use in my kitchen, so when I refer to a type of pan, grill, thermometer, etc., you'll know what I'm talking about.

Large Skillet: a 12-in/30-cm good-quality nonstick frying pan

Dutch Oven: a 6- to 8-qt/5.7- to 7.5-L stainless-steel or enameled cast-iron kettle

Medium Saucepan: a 2- to 3-qt/2- to 2.8-L stainless-steel saucepan

Outdoor Grill: a high-quality charcoal grill (It's no secret that I prefer the Big Green Egg.)

Broiler: the top heat source in a typical home oven with the pan set about 4 in/10 cm below the heat

Instant-Read Thermometer: the best on the market is a Superfast Thermapen

Knives: I use a very sharp 10-in/25-cm chef knife and a 6-in/15-cm boning knife for just about everything.

Spices: Unless I call for kosher salt, I use non-iodized table salt.

I use restaurant-grind black pepper.

Chili powder is one ingredient I *am* a snob about, and I buy San Antonio Red from Pendery's in Fort Worth, Texas. And as long as I'm ordering from them, I usually get my granulated onion, granulated garlic, and cumin from them too because their stuff is really fresh.

CHAPTER 2
The Classics

Any self-respecting collection of pork chop recipes needs to start with the classic preparations. We know them and we love them. Pork chops have been on most of our dinner tables all of our lives, no matter the culinary skill of our mothers. Panfried chops, breaded chops, baked chops with that stuff from the box shaken on them, and—on special occasions—grilled pork chops. Some of these may be fond memories of a special Sunday dinner at Grandma's or a favorite restaurant, and others may be more of a nightmare when Dad fired up the grill and created his new version of the blackened chop. But no matter, we all have a favorite pork chop dish and a story to go with it. In this chapter, I've given love and respect to the pork chop recipes that I consider to be the classics, but I've updated them to use the ways of the modern kitchen and a little good food science to get them cooked just right. My grandma never brined a chop and my dad never used an instant-read thermometer, but with a little help from those things we can re-create the classics and maybe even make them a little bit better.

CHICAGO-STYLE PORK CHOP SANDWICHES

In my days as a truck driver, I became very familiar with the street food of Chicago. One classic that doesn't get much attention is the Maxwell Street pork chop. Maxwell Street is the Sunday morning market, and the pork chops are cooked on a griddle next to a huge pile of sliced onions. The original uses bone-in chops, but boneless chops make the sandwich easier to manage. I'd serve these with homemade french fries.

¼ cup/60 ml vegetable oil, plus more if needed

2 very large yellow onions, halved and thinly sliced

1 tsp salt

1 tsp black pepper

6 boneless pork chops, about ½ in/12 mm thick

6 hamburger buns

In a large skillet over medium heat, warm the vegetable oil. Add the onions and season them with half of the salt and pepper. Toss to mix well and cook until they are soft and well browned, about 15 minutes. With a slotted spoon, transfer the onions to a bowl and set them aside.

Preheat the broiler on high. Season the chops with the remaining salt and pepper. Add a little more oil to the pan if needed, then raise the temperature to medium-high. Add the chops and cook for 3 to 4 minutes per side, until they are golden brown.

Under the broiler, toast the buns on the cut sides only, until lightly browned. On each bun, place a pork chop and then top it with one-sixth of the onions. Serve immediately.

SAUTÉED PORK CHOPS WITH APPLES

Pork chops and apples are a true classic combination, and I love to cook them together in the skillet. In this recipe I've added the classic seasonings of cinnamon, nutmeg, butter, and dried fruit to enhance that great cooked apple taste. I like to serve the chops with the apple mixture spooned over them and some simple green beans on the side.

¾ tsp salt

¼ tsp black pepper

½ tsp ground cinnamon

4 boneless pork chops, about ¾ in/2 cm thick

4 tbsp/55 g butter

3 large Gala apples, peeled, cored, and sliced ½ in/12 mm thick

2 tbsp dried cranberries

1 tbsp Sugar In The Raw

Pinch of ground nutmeg

In a small bowl, combine ½ tsp of the salt, the pepper, and ¼ tsp of the cinnamon. Mix well. Season the chops on all sides with all of the spice mixture.

Melt 2 tbsp of the butter in a large skillet over medium heat. Add the chops and cook for 4 to 5 minutes, until deep brown. Flip the chops and cook for 4 to 5 minutes more, until deep brown. Transfer the chops to a plate.

Add the remaining 2 tbsp butter to the pan. When the butter has melted, add the apples. Cook for 3 to 4 minutes, stirring and tossing occasionally, until they are lightly browned. Add the cranberries and mix well. Sprinkle the apples with the remaining ¼ tsp cinnamon, the remaining ¼ tsp salt, the sugar, and nutmeg. Toss well to coat evenly. Cook for 3 to 4 minutes, until the apples begin to soften.

Add the pork chops back to the pan, moving the apples to the sides. Cover the pan and cook for 3 to 4 minutes, until the chops are warmed through. Flip the chops and toss them with the apples. Cook for 3 to 4 minutes more, until the chops are cooked to an internal temperature of at least 150°F/65°C. Transfer the chops to a plate and spoon the apple mixture over the top before serving.

PINEAPPLE PORK CHOPS

Pork chops and pineapple go really well together in many ways. This dish combines them along with a sweet potato for a great-tasting combination that creates a nice side dish as a bonus. Always use fresh pineapple because the taste is completely different from the canned stuff, and if you'd like to add a little spice, a couple of minced jalapeños would be a great addition to this recipe.

¼ cup/30 g all-purpose flour

½ tsp paprika

1½ tsp salt

1 tsp black pepper

2 tbsp vegetable oil

4 boneless pork chops, about ¾ in/2 cm thick

2 tbsp butter

1 large sweet potato, peeled and cut into 1-in/2.5-cm cubes

2 cups/360 g coarsely chopped fresh pineapple

2 tbsp brown sugar

1½ tsp ground allspice

1 cup/240 ml chicken broth

On a flat plate, mix together the flour, paprika, ½ tsp of the salt, and ½ tsp of the pepper. Heat the vegetable oil in a large skillet over medium-high heat. Dredge the chops in the flour mixture, coating well on all sides. Shake off any excess. Place the chops in the pan and cook for about 4 minutes, until golden brown. Flip the chops and cook for another 4 minutes, until golden brown. Transfer the chops to a plate and set them aside.

Add the butter to the pan. When melted, add the sweet potato, pineapple, brown sugar, allspice, and remaining 1 tsp salt and ½ tsp pepper. Mix well with a large spoon. Cook for about 5 minutes, stirring occasionally, until the pineapple begins to soften. Add the broth and bring to a simmer. Add the pork chops back to the pan, working them down into the liquid. Return to a simmer. Reduce the heat, cover, and simmer for about 1 hour, stirring occasionally, until the pork chops are tender.

Transfer the chops to a large platter and tent loosely with foil. Raise the temperature to medium-high and cook the pineapple mixture for 3 to 4 minutes more, until most of the liquid is cooked off. With a slotted spoon, transfer the pineapple mixture to the platter next to the pork chops. Drizzle the remaining liquid over the pork chops, if desired, before serving.

BLACKENED PORK CHOPS

The classic blackening technique was created by Chef Paul Prudhomme in New Orleans for his dish of blackened redfish, but today just about anything with a spicy well-browned crust is known as "blackened." In the case of pork chops, that's a good thing because the kick from the cayenne and the well-browned edges make for a very delectable dinner. These are perfect with a side of Louisiana-style dirty rice.

1½ tsp salt

1 tsp paprika

½ tsp chili powder

½ tsp granulated garlic

½ tsp granulated onion

¼ tsp cayenne pepper

¼ tsp ground thyme

¼ tsp sugar

4 boneless pork chops, about ½ in/12 mm thick

¼ cup/55 g butter

In a small bowl, combine the salt, paprika, chili powder, granulated garlic, granulated onion, cayenne, thyme, and sugar. Mix well. Season the chops with the spice mixture, coating well on all sides.

Preheat a large heavy skillet over medium-high heat. Add half of the butter to the skillet and heat until it stops bubbling. Add two of the chops and cook for 3 to 4 minutes, until deeply browned. Flip and cook for another 3 to 4 minutes, until deeply browned and cooked to an internal temperature of 150°F/65°C. Transfer the cooked chops to a plate to rest.

Add the remaining 2 tbsp butter to the pan and repeat the process with the remaining chops. Transfer all the cooked chops to a plate to rest for 5 minutes before serving.

GARLIC LOVERS' PORK CHOPS

The name pretty much sums up this recipe. Only garlic lovers need read on. Garlic and pork chops are the stars and the garlic is heavy. But when you cook garlic, it mellows and sweetens, so the amount works well—as long as you *and* your date are both eating it. Homemade fettuccine alfredo on the side is the ideal companion to this garlicky dish.

¼ cup/30 g all-purpose flour

½ tsp paprika

1 tsp salt

1 tsp black pepper

4 bone-in pork chops, about ¾ in/2 cm thick

2 tbsp olive oil

½ cup/120 ml dry white wine

12 garlic cloves, crushed

6 to 8 scallions, white and firm green parts sliced

¼ cup/60 ml chicken broth

2 tbsp butter

⅓ cup/30 g chopped fresh parsley

On a flat plate, combine the flour, paprika, ½ tsp of the salt, and ½ tsp of the pepper. Dredge the chops in the flour mixture, coating well on all sides. Shake off any excess. Heat the olive oil in a large skillet over medium-high heat. Cook the chops for 3 to 4 minutes, until golden brown. Flip and cook for another 3 to 4 minutes, until golden brown. Transfer the chops to a plate and set aside.

Pour the wine into the pan to deglaze it, scraping the browned bits from the bottom. Add the garlic, scallions, broth, butter, and remaining ½ tsp salt and ½ tsp pepper. Mix well and cook for 2 to 3 minutes, until the scallions are soft. Add the parsley and mix well. Return the pork chops to the skillet and spoon some of the garlic mixture over the top. Reduce the heat to low and cover. Cook 3 minutes. Flip the chops and cover. Cook 3 to 4 minutes more, until the chops have reached an internal temperature of 150°F/65°C. Transfer the chops to a plate to rest for 5 minutes.

Raise the temperature to medium-high and cook the garlic mixture for about 3 minutes more, until most of the liquid has evaporated. Pour the garlic mixture over the chops to serve.

SKILLET-BRAISED PORK CHOPS WITH VIDALIA ONIONS

This is a dish I learned to make from my Grandma Julia a long time ago. It's a favorite at my house to this day. This recipe works well with end-cut chops that aren't very pretty but have a little bone and fat on them to add extra flavor to the pan gravy. This is perfect with buttered noodles and a side salad, just like Grandma used to serve.

6 bone-in pork chops, about ¾ in/2 cm thick

Salt

Black pepper

All-purpose flour

¼ cup/60 ml vegetable oil

2 cups/480 ml vegetable broth

1 tsp dried thyme

1 large Vidalia onion, halved and thinly sliced

Season the chops on both sides with salt and pepper, then dust each side with flour.

Add the vegetable oil to a large heavy skillet over medium-high heat. When the oil is hot, add the chops. Cook for 5 minutes, or until golden brown. Flip the chops and cook for another 5 minutes, or until golden brown. Drain off any excess oil from the skillet.

Mix 1 cup/240 ml of the broth with ½ tsp salt, 1 tsp pepper, and the thyme. Pour it over the chops. Spread the onion evenly over the top of the chops. When the liquid begins to boil, reduce the heat to a simmer. Cover the pan with a tight-fitting lid. Cook for 30 minutes, then check the level of liquid. There should be about ½ in/12 mm of liquid in the skillet. If it's low, add some of the reserved broth. Now flip the chops, placing them on top of the onion.

Replace the lid and cook for another 30 minutes, or until the chops are tender. Transfer them to a platter and tent loosely with foil. Raise the heat on the skillet and cook until the onion-liquid mixture is a creamy consistency. Season with salt if needed. Spoon the onion mixture over the pork chops to serve.

HERB AND PARMESAN-CRUSTED PORK CHOPS

These chops are panfried, kind of like Grandma used to make, but the breading has a fun twist with the addition of herbs and Parmesan cheese. Be sure to use freshly grated cheese in this recipe and any other that calls for grated Parmesan. The difference is well worth the trouble. Pasta tossed with basil pesto goes nicely with the herby chops.

4 bone-in pork chops, about ¾ in/2 cm thick

Salt

Black pepper

⅓ cup/40 g all-purpose flour, plus 2 tbsp

2 eggs

⅓ cup/35 g plain dried bread crumbs

⅓ cup/35 g freshly grated Parmesan cheese

½ tsp granulated garlic

½ tsp dried basil

½ tsp dried oregano

½ tsp dried thyme

⅓ cup/75 ml olive oil

Season the chops with salt and pepper and set them aside.

Put the ⅓ cup/40 g flour on a flat plate. Place the eggs and 1 tbsp water in a shallow bowl and mix well. Put the bread crumbs, Parmesan, remaining 2 tbsp flour, granulated garlic, basil, oregano, thyme, ½ tsp salt, and ½ tsp pepper on a flat plate and mix well.

Heat the olive oil in a large 12-in/30.5-cm skillet over medium heat. Dredge a chop in the flour, covering all sides. Shake off any excess. Dip it in the egg mixture, shaking off any excess. Dredge it in the bread-crumb mixture, covering all sides. Shake off any excess bread crumbs. Set the chop on a platter and repeat with the others.

Place the chops in the hot skillet and cook for 6 to 7 minutes, until golden brown. Flip the chops and cook for 6 to 7 minutes more, until they reach an internal temperature of 150°F/65°C. Transfer them to a platter covered with paper towels and let them rest for 5 minutes before serving.

HONEY-BRINED PECAN-CRUSTED PORK CHOPS

This recipe comes from my old barbecue-contest buddy Fast Eddy Maurin. We've both been involved in the barbecue world for a long time. Eddy builds and cooks on his own line of pellet grills and smokers, so it's no surprise that he cooks his chops kind of slow on the grill. I asked him for a brined recipe and he went way beyond that for this great dish. I'd serve these with a simple baked potato.

BRINE

¼ cup/60 g kosher salt

¼ cup/50 g sugar

¼ cup/85 g clover honey

12 to 15 stems fresh rosemary

4 bone-in pork chops, about ¾ in/2 cm thick

½ cup/120 ml balsamic vinegar

¼ cup/80 g blackberry jam

¼ cup/50 g sugar

¼ cup/30 g finely chopped pecans

2 tbsp paprika

2 tbsp seasoned salt

1 tbsp granulated garlic

1½ tsp granulated onion

1½ tsp ground allspice

1½ tsp ground cumin

1½ tsp black pepper

TO MAKE THE BRINE: The day before you plan to cook, combine 1 qt/1 L water, the salt, sugar, honey, and rosemary in a medium saucepan. Mix well and place over medium-high heat. Cook, stirring often, until the salt and sugar are well blended with the water. Transfer the brine to a bowl and refrigerate until cold, at least 4 hours.

Place the chops in a large zip-top bag and pour the brine over them. Seal the bag, removing as much air as possible. Refrigerate for about 24 hours.

Prepare an outdoor grill to cook direct over medium heat. Combine the vinegar and jam in a small saucepan over low heat. Cook, stirring occasionally, until thickened, 20 to 30 minutes. Remove from the heat and let rest.

Remove the chops from the brine and rinse well. Dry the chops and set aside. In the bowl of a food processor with the metal blade, combine the sugar, pecans, paprika, seasoned salt, granulated garlic, granulated onion, allspice, cumin, and pepper. Process until the mixture is finely ground, about 30 seconds. Transfer the sugar mixture to a flat plate. Dredge the chops in the sugar mixture, coating well on all sides. Shake off any excess. Place the chops on the grill and cook for 4 to 5 minutes, until golden brown. Flip the chops and cook for 4 to 5 minutes more, until golden brown and cooked to an internal temperature of 150°F/65°C. Transfer the chops to a platter and drizzle them with the balsamic glaze. Let them rest for 5 minutes before serving.

HOMEMADE TERIYAKI PORK CHOPS

The bold taste of homemade teriyaki is a classic combination with pork chops. The indoor broiler will do the job too if you can't get outside, but cooking them on the outdoor grill adds an extra dimension to the flavor. White rice would go great with these, but I like to add grilled pineapple rings along with a garnish of thinly sliced scallions.

4 bone-in pork chops, about ¾ in/2 cm thick

¾ cup/180 ml soy sauce

½ cup/120 ml pineapple juice

⅓ cup/65 g brown sugar

4 garlic cloves, crushed

2 tbsp minced fresh ginger

1 tbsp sesame oil

1 tbsp Sriracha hot sauce (optional)

Place the pork chops in a large zip-top bag and set them aside. In a medium bowl, combine the soy sauce, pineapple juice, brown sugar, garlic, ginger, sesame oil, and hot sauce (if using). Mix well. Pour over the pork chops. Seal the bag, removing as much air as possible. Refrigerate for at least 8 hours and preferably a whole day.

Prepare an outdoor grill to cook direct over medium heat. Remove the chops from the marinade and place them directly on the grill. Cook for 4 to 5 minutes, until golden brown. Flip and cook for 4 to 5 minutes more, until the chops reach an internal temperature of 150°F/65°C. Transfer them to a platter and cover loosely with foil. Let them rest for 5 minutes before serving.

GRILLED PORK CHOPS WITH HOMEMADE BBQ SAUCE

Grilled pork chops definitely fit in with the classics, and at many houses they're the absolute favorite meal from the grill. The smoky pork taste combined with the caramelized sweet-sticky barbecue sauce is an awesome combination, and when you make the sauce from scratch, it really takes it to the next level. Potato salad and corn on the cob are perfect backyard dinner partners.

SAUCE

2 tbsp vegetable oil

½ red onion, finely chopped

2 garlic cloves, crushed

1 jalapeño, seeded and minced

1 cup/240 g ketchup

¼ cup/60 ml vinegar

¼ cup/85 g honey

¼ cup/50 g firmly packed brown sugar

¼ tsp salt

¼ tsp black pepper

6 bone-in pork chops, about 1 in/2.5 cm thick

Salt

Black pepper

Paprika

TO MAKE THE SAUCE: Heat the vegetable oil in a medium saucepan over medium heat. Add the onion, garlic, and jalapeño and mix well. Cook for about 5 minutes, until the onion is soft. Add ¼ cup/60 ml water, the ketchup, vinegar, honey, brown sugar, salt, and pepper. Mix well. Bring the sauce to a low simmer. Reduce the heat, cover, and cook for about 15 minutes, stirring occasionally, until the sauce begins to thicken. Remove it from the heat and set aside.

Prepare an outdoor grill to cook direct over medium heat. Season the chops with salt, pepper, and paprika. Place them directly on the cooking grate and cook for 3 to 4 minutes, until golden brown. Flip the chops and brush the top with a heavy coat of the barbecue sauce. Cook for another 3 to 4 minutes, until golden brown on the bottom. Flip the chops and brush the top with a heavy coat of sauce. Continue cooking, flipping, and brushing with sauce about every 2 minutes, until the sauce is cooked on the chops and they have reached an internal temperature of 150°F/65°C. Transfer the chops to a platter to rest for 5 minutes before serving.

SOUTHERN-FRIED PORK CHOPS

This recipe is from my friend Marsha Hale from Lynchburg, Tennessee. I always include a recipe from Marsha in my books because I love her true Southern cooking. These simple skillet-fried chops are another winner. They are crispy and delicious, especially with greens and cornbread.

1 cup/130 g all-purpose flour

2 tbsp cornstarch

1 tsp garlic powder

½ tsp salt

½ tsp paprika

½ tsp onion powder

¼ tsp black pepper

¼ tsp white pepper

1 egg

¼ cup/60 ml buttermilk

Cooking oil for frying

4 bone-in pork chops, about ½ in/12 mm thick

In a small bowl, combine the flour, cornstarch, garlic powder, salt, paprika, onion powder, and both peppers. Mix well and set aside. Break the egg into a shallow bowl. Add the buttermilk and whisk with a fork until well combined.

Pour about ½ in/12 mm oil into a large cast-iron skillet over medium heat. (Test the oil by adding a pinch of flour. It should sizzle when the oil is ready.) Dredge a chop in the flour mixture, covering all sides. Shake off any excess. Dip it in the egg mixture, shaking off any excess. Dredge it again in the flour mixture and coat the sides well. Shake off any excess flour. Set the chop on a platter and repeat with the others.

Add the chops one at a time to the hot cooking oil. Cook for 4 to 5 minutes, until the chops are golden brown on the bottom. Flip them over. Cook for 4 to 5 minutes more, until the chops are golden brown on the bottom and have reached an internal temperature of 150°F/65°C. Let them rest for 5 minutes before serving.

DRY-RUBBED IOWA CHOPS

Many Iowans are involved in the pork industry, so it's no surprise that they love pork chops. There's even a cut named after the state, and it's a good one. The Iowa chop is a bone-in chop at least 1¼ in/3 cm thick. That makes them perfect for grilling with just a simple dry rub to bring out that great pork flavor. Fresh corn on the cob is a good accompaniment.

1 tbsp salt

1½ tsp black pepper

1 tsp granulated garlic

1 tsp onion powder

1 tsp lemon pepper

1 tsp Sugar In The Raw

1 tsp paprika

4 bone-in pork rib chops, about 1½ in/4 cm thick

Prepare an outdoor grill to cook direct over medium heat.

In a small bowl, combine the salt, pepper, garlic, onion powder, lemon pepper, sugar, and paprika. Mix well. Sprinkle half of the mixture on one side of the chops. Let rest for 5 minutes. Flip the chops and sprinkle the opposite sides with the remaining rub. Let rest for 5 minutes.

Transfer the chops to the grill. Cook for 5 to 6 minutes, until golden brown. Flip the chops and cook for another 6 minutes, until golden brown and cooked to an internal temperature of 150°F/65°C. Transfer the chops to a platter and tent loosely with aluminum foil. Let them rest for 5 minutes before serving.

STAND-UP STUFFED PORK CHOPS WITH BACON AND BLUE CHEESE

SERVES 4

These chops are unique, as they are served standing on their sides with the beautiful stuffing mounding out of the middle. If you're not comfortable making the cut to open the side, just ask the butcher to do it for you. The stuffing is rich and hearty, so I accompany these with a simple side salad dressed with a light vinaigrette.

RUB

1 tsp salt

1 tsp paprika

½ tsp black pepper

½ tsp granulated garlic

4 boneless pork chops, about 1½ in/4 cm thick

2 tbsp olive oil

STUFFING

6 slices bacon, cooked and crumbled

½ cup/50 g crumbled blue cheese

¼ cup/30 g grated Parmesan cheese

¼ cup/30 g panko or bread crumbs

2 tbsp butter, melted

½ tsp black pepper

¼ tsp granulated garlic

Preheat the oven to 350°F/180°C.

TO MAKE THE RUB: In a small bowl, combine the salt, paprika, pepper, and granulated garlic. Mix well and set aside.

With a sharp knife, cut a pocket in the fatty side of each pork chop, leaving the ends intact but cutting deeply into the middle. Be careful not to cut all the way through or the stuffing will leak out. Rub the chops liberally with the olive oil. Sprinkle the rub all over the chops inside and out, using it all.

TO MAKE THE STUFFING: In a medium bowl, combine the bacon, blue cheese, Parmesan, panko, butter, pepper, and granulated garlic.

Lay the chops down on the uncut sides with the pockets facing up and opened. Fill each chop with one-fourth of the stuffing. Coat a baking sheet with vegetable spray and transfer the chops to it, setting them in the stand-up position. Bake the chops for 25 minutes, or until the stuffing is lightly browned and the chops have reached an internal temperature of 150°F/65°C. Let them rest for 5 minutes before serving.

CHAPTER 3
Fresh Ideas

When most of us think about pork chops, we think about thick slabs of meat with a big sauce or gravy and an overall hearty meal. These days, we don't always want to sit down to a big meal, but we don't want to give up our favorite foods either. The good news is that pork chops for our generation are lean and healthful and they come in many shapes and sizes, so they don't always have to be the big bold center of the plate. In this chapter, I've broken down the stereotype and added pork chops to some dishes where they are usually forgotten. Pork chops in a salad? Sure, why not! Everyone likes a little something on top of their salad and a broiled pork chop is a great choice. It's lean, healthful, and delicious! I think pork chops are an easy addition to dishes like a tortilla wrap with spinach, a flat bread pizza, or—for the carb counters—a trendy and tasty lettuce wrap. I've replaced the heavy sauces with fresh fruit combos and a balsamic glaze that'll rival any sweet-sticky barbecue sauce. I've used the broiler a lot in this chapter and, of course, the outdoor grill is an obvious substitute for that. These recipes are a great way to healthy up your whole family's diet while still giving them the great taste of pork chops.

GRILLED ROMAINE AND PORK CHOPPED SALAD

If you saw my appearance on *Chopped Grill-masters* on the Food Network, this recipe may look familiar. But with the addition of pork chops, it becomes a much more tasty and complete dish. Feel free to add any vegetables that you like to grill. Grilled garlic bread is the logical choice to serve alongside.

DRESSING

½ cup/120 ml sweet barbecue sauce

¼ cup/60 ml olive oil

2 tbsp apple cider vinegar

2 tbsp apple juice

1 tbsp honey

2 garlic cloves, crushed

½ tsp salt

¼ tsp black pepper

4 boneless pork chops, about ½ in/12 mm thick

Olive oil

Salt

Black pepper

3 large romaine crowns, split in half lengthwise

1 small red onion, quartered

1 small red bell pepper, cut into quarters

1 ear corn, shucked

½ English cucumber, cut into quarters lengthwise

½ cup/40 g freshly grated Parmesan cheese

Prepare an outdoor grill to cook direct over medium-high heat.

TO MAKE THE DRESSING: In a medium bowl, combine the barbecue sauce, olive oil, vinegar, apple juice, honey, garlic, salt, and pepper. Whisk vigorously to blend and set aside.

Brush the chops lightly with olive oil and season with salt and pepper. Brush the romaine, onion, bell pepper, corn, and cucumber lightly with oil and season with salt and pepper. Place the chops on the grill and cook for 4 to 5 minutes, until golden brown. Flip and cook another 4 to 5 minutes, until they reach an internal temperature of 150°F/65°C. Transfer them to a plate and set aside.

Put the onion, bell pepper, corn, and cucumber on the grill. Cook for 3 to 4 minutes, until lightly charred. Flip and cook for another 3 to 4 minutes, until lightly charred. Leave the corn on until it's lightly charred on all sides. As the vegetables are done, transfer them to a plate and set aside. Place the romaine halves on the grill, cut-side down, and cook for 4 to 5 minutes, until lightly browned. Flip and cook another 2 to 4 minutes, until lightly browned and wilted. Transfer the romaine to a plate and set aside.

continued

With a sharp knife, cut the chops into bite-size pieces and set aside. Cut the onion, bell pepper, and cucumber into large dice and set aside. Cut the kernels from the ear of corn and set aside. Split the romaine halves down the middle, then chop them into bite-size pieces. Place the romaine in a large salad bowl. Add the pork chops, onion, bell pepper, corn, and cucumber. Whisk the dressing well again and pour half of it over the salad. Toss well. Add half of the remaining dressing and the Parmesan and toss well. Add the rest of the dressing if desired and check for salt and pepper; add if needed. Toss well before serving.

PORK CHOP AND MIXED GREENS SALAD WITH RASPBERRY VINAIGRETTE

The delicate flavor of raspberry pairs beautifully with many things, and when it's infused into vinaigrette, it's about as good as it gets. I've used mixed greens here with sunflower seeds for a little crunch, but feel free to mix it up using your own salad favorites. A toasted English muffin on the side is a nice accompaniment.

DRESSING

¾ cup/255 g seedless raspberry jam

½ cup/120 ml seasoned rice vinegar

2 tbsp olive oil

1 tbsp agave nectar

½ tsp salt

½ tsp black pepper

¼ tsp dried marjoram

2 boneless pork chops, about ¾ in/2 cm thick

Salt

Black pepper

4 cups/200 g mixed salad greens, such as mesclun, arugula, red leaf, romaine, and baby spinach

1 cup/70 g julienned carrots

½ cup/50 g sliced scallions, white and green parts

⅓ cup/40 g shelled sunflower seeds

TO MAKE THE DRESSING: In a blender, combine the jam, vinegar, olive oil, agave, salt, pepper, and marjoram. Blend on high for about 45 seconds, until frothy.

Season the chops with salt and pepper. Place the chops in a zip-top bag and pour ½ cup/120 ml of the dressing over them. Refrigerate them for at least 1 hour and up to 4 hours.

Preheat the broiler on high, with the rack about 5 in/ 12 cm from the heat. Remove the chops from the bag and place them on a broiler pan. Broil for 5 to 6 minutes, until golden brown. Flip and broil for 5 to 6 minutes more, until they reach an internal temperature of 150°F/65°C. Transfer them to a plate and set aside.

In a large salad bowl, toss the greens. Add the carrots, scallions, and sunflower seeds. Toss well. Add half of the remaining dressing and toss well. Add more dressing if desired and toss again. Slice the pork chops thinly. Place a quarter of the salad on each of four plates and top each with pork chop slices. Drizzle additional dressing over the pork chops, if desired, before serving.

SANDI'S ASIAN-INSPIRED PORK CHOP SALAD

Sandi is the love of my life and she really likes Vietnamese food. So when I asked her to help me with an Asian-inspired salad, she was all over it. She brought home samples of her favorite sauce and asked her Asian friends for help. When it was all said and done, she had created a great salad. I'd serve this all by itself with hot tea to drink.

4 boneless pork chops, about ⅜ in/1 cm thick

MARINADE

3 tbsp soy sauce

2 tbsp hoisin sauce

1 tbsp oyster sauce

1 garlic clove, crushed

½ tsp sesame oil

¼ tsp white pepper

DRESSING

3 tbsp freshly squeezed lime juice

3 tbsp sugar

2 tbsp peanut oil

2 tbsp fish sauce

1 tbsp Thai chili sauce

5 cups/140 g baby spinach and spring greens mix

2 cups/140 g shredded broccoli

1 cup/70 g julienned carrots

1 cup/120 g julienned jícama

Salt

1 cup/60 g chow mein noodles

½ cup/40 g thinly sliced scallion tops

Place the chops in a medium zip-top bag.

TO MAKE THE MARINADE: In a small bowl, combine 1 tbsp water, the soy sauce, hoisin sauce, oyster sauce, garlic, sesame oil, and pepper. Using a whisk, mix the marinade well. Pour the marinade over the chops. Seal the bag, pressing out as much air as possible. Refrigerate for at least 1 hour and up to 4 hours.

Preheat the broiler on high, with the rack about 6 in/ 15 cm from the heat. Remove the chops from the marinade and place them on a rimmed baking sheet. Broil for 3 to 4 minutes, until the chops are golden brown. Flip the chops and broil for 3 to 4 minutes more, until golden brown and cooked to an internal temperature of 150°F/65°C. Remove the pan from the broiler and transfer the chops to a plate to cool.

Combine ½ cup/120 ml water, the lime juice, sugar, peanut oil, fish sauce, and chili sauce in a blender. Blend on high for 30 seconds, until frothy.

Cut the pork chops in half lengthwise and then slice them thinly. In a large salad bowl, combine the spinach mix, broccoli, carrots, and jicama. Toss well. Drizzle with three-fourths of the dressing and toss well. Add the pork chops and toss well. Check for salt and add if needed. Add the remaining dressing if needed. Toss well. Add the noodles and scallion tops and toss well before serving.

PORK CHOP TACO SALAD WITH AVOCADO DRESSING

Pork chops get a lot of love in this upside-down taco salad. I call it upside down because the chips are crushed and sprinkled on the top for a little bit of crunch in every bite. For extra flavor, try cooking the chops on the grill. Salsa would be a nice additional topping and, for you fire eaters, just add an extra jalapeño to the mix. I'd serve this with a cold *cerveza*.

1 tsp salt

1 tsp black pepper

1 tsp chili powder

1 tsp ground cumin

4 boneless pork chops, ½ in/12 mm thick

DRESSING

2 ripe Hass avocados, cut into quarters

½ cup/120 ml sour cream

½ cup/120 ml mayonnaise

¼ cup/20 g coarsely chopped fresh cilantro

½ lime, juiced

2 garlic cloves, crushed

½ jalapeño, seeded and chopped

½ tsp salt

½ tsp black pepper

2 tbsp milk (optional)

1 head iceberg lettuce, thinly sliced

2 ears corn, kernels cut from the cob

4 large Roma tomatoes, seeded and chopped

1 cup/115 g finely shredded Jack cheese

1 cup/115 g finely shredded mild Cheddar cheese

½ red onion, thinly sliced

2 cups/140 g crushed tortilla chips

Fresh cilantro for garnish

Preheat the broiler on high, with the rack 5 to 6 in/12 to 15 cm from the heat.

In a small bowl, combine the salt, pepper, chili powder, and cumin. Season the chops liberally with the spice mix. Place the chops on a broiler pan and cook for 6 minutes, until well browned. Flip the chops and cook for another 6 minutes, until they're well browned and have reached an internal temperature of at least 150°F/65°C. Transfer them to a plate and set aside.

TO MAKE THE DRESSING: Put the avocados, sour cream, mayonnaise, cilantro, lime juice, garlic, jalapeño, salt, and pepper in a blender. Blend on high, scraping down the sides as needed, for about 1 minute, until smooth. If the dressing is too thick, add 1 or 2 tbsp milk and blend for another 15 seconds. Transfer to a bowl and set aside.

In a large salad bowl, combine the lettuce, corn kernels, tomatoes, both cheeses, and onion. Toss well to mix. Cut the pork chops into ½-in/12-mm cubes and add them to the top of the salad, spreading them evenly. Sprinkle the crushed chips over the salad, spreading them evenly. Drizzle two-thirds of the dressing over the top of the salad, spreading it evenly. Reserve the remaining dressing to serve on the side. Garnish the salad with a few cilantro leaves. When the guests are ready to eat, toss the salad well with the reserved dressing on the side.

PORK CHOP WRAPS WITH SPINACH AND FETA CHEESE

The feta mixed with the cream cheese and black olives makes a great spread with big flavors to get this wrap started. Add in a pork chop and spinach and everybody is going to want to try these. You can cut them in half for lunch or slice them thinly into pinwheels for a creative and tasty appetizer. All this needs is a few fresh sliced tomatoes to make a meal.

2 boneless pork chops, about ¾ in/2 cm thick

Salt

Black pepper

Granulated garlic

½ cup/115 g cream cheese, at room temperature

½ cup/75 g crumbled feta cheese

¼ cup/30 g finely chopped red onion

2 tbsp finely chopped black olives

Four 10-in/25-cm flour tortillas

1 cup/30 g baby spinach leaves

Preheat the broiler on high, with the rack 5 to 6 in/ 12 to 15 cm from the heat. Season the chops with salt, pepper, and granulated garlic. Place the chops on a broiler pan or baking sheet and cook for 5 minutes, until golden brown. Flip and cook for 5 minutes more, until they reach an internal temperature of 150°F/65°C. Transfer them to a plate to cool. When the chops are cooled, slice them thinly and set aside.

In a medium bowl, combine the cream cheese and feta. Mix well. Add the onion and olives. Mix well. Spread the cream cheese mixture over two-thirds of each tortilla, leaving one-third plain so the edge won't be messy to eat when rolled up. Lay the spinach leaves on the cream cheese mixture, doubling them up if necessary. Lay the slices of pork chop over the spinach in a single layer, dividing them equally among the tortillas. Starting on the full side, roll up the tortillas as tightly as possible. Lay each wrap with the flap on the bottom to help hold it together. When ready to serve, cut each one in half on the diagonal to serve as a sandwich or slice ¾ in/2 cm thick to serve as pinwheels.

SPICY PORK CHOP LETTUCE WRAPS

Lettuce wraps are all the trendy rage, but they get even better when there is a pork chop involved. It's a great way to eat low-carb and high-flavor. I've used Boston lettuce, but you can substitute Bibb lettuce or even romaine for the wrapper. If you like it all a little spicier, you can drizzle on some Thai chili sauce. Cut up some fresh fruit and serve it on the side.

3 boneless pork chops, about ¾ in/2 cm thick

Salt

Black pepper

1 tbsp olive oil

6 to 8 scallions, sliced thinly on the diagonal

1 garlic clove, crushed

1 tsp finely chopped fresh ginger

2 tbsp chicken broth

1½ tbsp soy sauce

1½ tbsp oyster sauce

2 tsp *sambal oelek* (a spicy chili paste found in the Asian foods aisle)

2 Roma tomatoes, seeded and diced

1 cup/70 g julienned carrots

½ lime, juiced

8 medium Boston lettuce leaves, rinsed, patted dry

Preheat the broiler on high, with the rack 5 to 6 in/ 12 to 15 cm from the heat. Season the chops with salt and pepper. Place the chops on a broiler pan or baking sheet and cook for 5 minutes, until golden brown. Flip and cook for 5 minutes more, until they reach an internal temperature of 150°F/65°C. Transfer them to a plate to cool. When the chops are cooled, cut them into ½-in/12-mm dice.

Heat the olive oil in a medium skillet over medium-high heat. Add the cut-up pork chops and mix well. Cook for 2 minutes, stirring occasionally, until the pork begins to brown. Add the scallions, garlic, and ginger. Cook for 2 minutes, stirring occasionally, until the scallions begin to soften. In a small bowl, mix together the broth, soy sauce, oyster sauce, and *sambal oelek*. Pour half of the broth mixture into the pan and mix well. Add the tomatoes and carrots and mix well. Cook for 2 minutes, stirring occasionally, until well blended and the carrots just begin to soften. Drizzle the lime juice over the pork chop mixture and mix well. Remove from the heat and divide the mixture evenly among the lettuce leaves. Serve the reserved sauce on the side to drizzle as desired.

PORK CHOP AND VEGGIE STIR-FRY

Pork chops can be really lean, so when you combine them with pea pods and broccoli florets you're on track to make something that's delicious and good for you. The daikon (Japanese radish) adds an interesting texture and flavor too. The whole family loves a big stir-fry, and with this one you can feel good about serving them something healthful.

3 boneless pork chops, about ½ in/12 mm thick

Salt

Black pepper

½ cup/120 ml peanut oil

2 celery stalks, sliced thinly on the diagonal

3 medium carrots, sliced thinly on the diagonal

2 cups/150 g sliced mushrooms

3 garlic cloves, crushed

1 tbsp minced fresh ginger

1 cup/110 g julienned daikon

6 to 8 scallions, white and green parts sliced thinly on the diagonal

1 cup/110 g pea pods

2 cups/110 g broccoli florets

¼ cup/60 ml vegetable broth

3 tbsp soy sauce

Season the pork chops with salt and pepper. Heat a large wok or Dutch oven over medium-high heat. Add ¼ cup/60 ml of the peanut oil and heat until smoking. Add the pork chops and cook for 3 to 4 minutes, until golden brown. Flip the chops and cook for 3 to 4 minutes more, until golden brown and cooked to an internal temperature of 150°F/65°C. Transfer them to a plate lined with paper towels.

Add the remaining ¼ cup/60 ml oil to the pan and let it get hot. Add the celery and carrots and cook, stirring occasionally, for 3 to 4 minutes, until the celery begins to soften. Add the mushrooms, garlic, and ginger and toss well. Cook for 3 to 4 minutes, until the mushrooms begin to soften. Add the daikon and scallions and toss well. Cook for 1 minute. Add the pea pods and broccoli and toss well. Cook for 3 to 4 minutes, until the broccoli begins to wilt. In a small bowl, mix together the broth, soy sauce, ¼ tsp salt, and ½ tsp pepper. Pour the broth mixture over the vegetables and toss well. Slice the pork chops thinly on the diagonal. Add the pork to the wok and toss to mix well. Cook for 2 to 3 minutes, tossing occasionally to blend the flavors. Check for salt and pepper and add if necessary. Serve immediately.

FLAT BREAD
PORK CHOP PIZZA

There are a lot of flat-bread choices in the super-market these days, and they are all fun to cook with. My favorite is Indian naan, a free-form light pocket bread. Using these makes a much lighter pizza with tons of flavor. Go easy on the toppings and you'll have something that's healthful and delicious at the same time. Add a simple side salad and you've come up with a quick week-night meal.

2 boneless pork chops, about ½ in/12 mm thick

Salt

Black pepper

Paprika

2 pieces flat bread or naan, about 7 in/17 cm across

¼ cup/60 ml olive oil

2 large garlic cloves, sliced very thin

8 grape tomatoes, sliced

¼ tsp dried oregano

4 oz/115 g Brie cheese, thinly sliced

Preheat the broiler on high, with the rack 5 to 6 in/12 to 15 cm from the heat. Season the pork chops on both sides with salt, pepper, and paprika. Place the chops on a pan and broil for 3 to 4 minutes, until golden brown. Flip the chops and cook for 3 minutes more, until they reach an internal temperature of 150°F/65°C. Transfer them to a plate and set aside to cool.

Preheat the oven to 400°F/200°C. Place the flat breads on a baking sheet. In a small skillet over medium heat, warm the olive oil. Add the garlic and cook, stirring occasionally, until soft. Add the tomatoes and oregano and mix well. Cook for 1 minute, then remove from the heat. Spoon the garlic mixture evenly over the flat breads. Season with salt and pepper. Slice the pork chops very thinly. Lay the slices on top of the garlic mixture, spreading evenly. Top with the sliced Brie, spreading evenly. Bake for 15 minutes, until the cheese is melted and the crust is golden brown. Transfer the pizzas to a board. Let them rest for 2 minutes before slicing each pizza into six pieces and serving.

PORK CHOPS WITH BROCCOLI

Lean and healthful boneless pork chops are a perfect match for fresh and vitamin-rich broccoli florets. This is definitely not what you would expect from a pork chop skillet dinner, but it's delicious and good for you, and your family will love it. A crisp salad is a nice side and fresh fruit for dessert doesn't hurt either.

4 boneless pork chops, about ¾ in/2 cm thick

Salt

Black pepper

Paprika

¼ cup/60 ml olive oil

4 cups/220 g broccoli florets

½ cup/35 g julienned carrots

3 garlic cloves, crushed

1 cup/240 ml chicken broth

¼ cup/30 g grated Parmesan cheese

Season the chops with salt, pepper, and paprika on all sides. Heat half of the olive oil in a large skillet over medium-high heat. Add the chops to the skillet and cook for 3 to 4 minutes, until golden brown. Flip the chops and cook for another 3 to 4 minutes, until golden brown. Transfer the chops to a plate and set aside.

Add the remaining oil to the pan. Add the broccoli, carrots, and garlic. Season with salt and pepper. Mix well and cook for 3 to 4 minutes, until the broccoli begins to soften. Add the broth and mix well. Place the chops on top of the broccoli. Cover and cook for 3 minutes. Flip the chops and work them down into the broccoli mixture. Cover and cook for 3 to 4 minutes more, until the broccoli is al dente and the chops are cooked to an internal temperature of 150°F/65°C.

Transfer the chops to a large platter and place the broccoli next to them. Sprinkle the cheese over the chops and the broccoli, and let rest for 5 minutes before serving.

BALSAMIC AND VANILLA-GLAZED PORK CHOPS

A balsamic glaze is a natural for grilled pork chops, but for this one I wanted something a little different. I was thinking something that would seem like a barbecue sauce, but without all the sugar and tomato making it so heavy. Vanilla with a bit of agave nectar and balsamic worked well, and the combination changes all three ingredients into one unique flavor. Try serving this with baked sweet potatoes just to shake things up.

GLAZE

2 cups/480 ml balsamic vinegar

¼ cup/60 ml agave nectar

1 tsp vanilla extract

¼ tsp salt

¼ tsp black pepper

4 boneless pork chops, about 1 in/2.5 cm thick

Salt

Black pepper

TO MAKE THE GLAZE: In a medium saucepan over low heat, bring the balsamic vinegar to a simmer. Cook for about 1 hour, until reduced to about ½ cup/120 ml. Remove from the heat. Add the agave, vanilla, salt, and pepper. Mix well and set aside. (This may be done a few days ahead. Just transfer the glaze to a covered container and refrigerate.)

Prepare an outdoor grill to cook direct over medium heat. Season the pork chops liberally with salt and pepper. Place the chops directly on the cooking grate and cook for 2 minutes, until the outside has a light color. Flip and brush the top with a light coating of the glaze. Cook another 2 minutes and flip. Brush the top with a light coating of the glaze. Continue cooking, flipping, and brushing with the glaze until the chops are dark brown and have reached an internal temperature of 150°F/65°C, 9 to 10 minutes total.

Transfer the chops to a plate and tent loosely with aluminum foil. Let them rest for 5 minutes before serving. Discard any leftover glaze.

BROILED PORK CHOPS WITH PINEAPPLE CHUTNEY

SERVES 4

Chutney is a condiment typically made with fruit, vegetables, and spices. It can be served chunky or smooth. For this one I've used fresh pineapple, onion, garlic, and a jalapeño and I've left it chunky. If you like your chutney spicy, add another jalapeño, and if you like it smooth, just throw it in the food processor for a bit. The sweetness of the chutney goes well with a side of rice pilaf.

4 bone-in pork chops, about ¾ in/2 cm thick

Salt

Black pepper

Paprika

2 tbsp olive oil

½ cup/60 g minced red onion

1 jalapeño, seeded and minced

1 garlic clove, crushed

2 cups/360 g ½-in/12-mm dice fresh pineapple

¼ cup/60 ml apple cider vinegar

1 tsp honey

Season the pork chops with salt, pepper, and paprika and set aside.

Heat the olive oil in a large skillet over medium heat. Add the onion, jalapeño, and garlic. Cook until the onion is soft, about 10 minutes. Add the pineapple and vinegar. Reduce the heat to low and simmer for 15 minutes. Stir in the honey. Keep warm.

Preheat the broiler on high, with the rack 5 to 6 in/ 12 to 15 cm from the heat. Place the chops on a pan and broil for 4 to 5 minutes, until golden brown. Flip the chops and cook for 4 to 5 minutes more, until golden brown and cooked to an internal temperature of 150°F/65°C. Transfer them to a platter to rest for 5 minutes before serving with the warm chutney on the side.

PORK CHOPS WITH FRESH MANGO-HABANERO SALSA

Mango salsa has many lives and can be transformed to accompany anything from a bowl of chips to a bowl of ice cream and just about everything in between. When you add the heat of a habanero to the salsa, it becomes a great topping for a grilled pork chop. The sweet mango countered by the spicy habanero topping the smoky pork chop combines all of my favorite food groups. A little homemade coleslaw on the side will tone down the heat from the chile.

SALSA

1 mango, cut into small dice

2 Roma tomatoes, seeded and cut into small dice

6 to 8 scallions, white and some of the green parts sliced thinly

½ habanero chile, seeded and minced
(Add more if you dare! These are really hot!)

2 garlic cloves, crushed

2 tbsp minced fresh cilantro

½ lime, juiced

¼ tsp salt

¼ tsp black pepper

4 bone-in pork chops, about ¾ in/2 cm thick

Salt

Black pepper

Paprika

TO MAKE THE SALSA: Combine the mango, tomatoes, scallions, habanero, and garlic in a medium bowl. Mix well. Add the cilantro, lime juice, salt, and pepper and mix well. Set the salsa aside at room temperature for 30 minutes, stirring occasionally.

Preheat the broiler on high, with the rack 5 to 6 in/ 12 to 15 cm from the heat. Season the pork chops on both sides with salt, pepper, and paprika. Place the chops on a pan and broil for 4 to 5 minutes, until golden brown. Flip the chops and cook for 4 to 5 minutes more, until golden brown and cooked to an internal temperature of 150°F/65°C.

Transfer them to a platter to rest for 5 minutes before serving them with the chutney on the side.

When the weather is cool or you've had a long tough day, nothing can soothe your soul like a big bowl of soup or a heaping scoop of a casserole fresh from the oven. The wonderful communal vibe when the one big pot comes to the middle of the table for all to share makes us feel warm and fuzzy inside. But pork chops have been left out of the party like an ugly duckling . . . until now. I say pork chop and noodle soup is even better than the common type that shall remain nameless. And pork chop gumbo is as good as it gets, but nobody has ever heard of it. It's like a conspiracy against pork chops. Maybe it's because pork chops are so good just cooked simply, but they're also good when used in these slow-cooked family-style dishes. I like to brown the chops ahead and cut them up for a great pot of chili. And the flavor a few bone-in pork chops add to a pot of white beans will change your life. So let's stop the injustice against pork chops now, and give them their place in our favorite slow-cooked one-pot dishes.

PORK CHOP POT ROAST

Everybody loves pot roast, with that rich gravy and the soft carrots and onions flavoring the meat. When you switch to thick-cut pork chops, your pot roast gets leaner, more economical, and even tastier than the original. This version is so good you'll want to serve it to company. I skip the potatoes in the pot and serve it over roasted garlic mashed potatoes.

2 tbsp vegetable oil

½ cup/55 g all-purpose flour, plus 2 tbsp

1½ tsp salt

¾ tsp black pepper

4 boneless pork chops, about 1½ in/4 cm thick

1 yellow onion, diced

2 garlic cloves, crushed

½ tsp dried basil

1 bay leaf

8 carrots, peeled and cut into 2-in/5-cm pieces

1 cup/240 ml vegetable broth

½ cup/120 ml tomato sauce

½ cup/120 ml red wine

Preheat the oven to 350°F/180°C. Heat the vegetable oil in a Dutch oven over medium-high heat.

On a flat plate, combine the ½ cup/55 g flour with 1 tsp of the salt and ½ tsp of the pepper. Dredge the chops in the flour, coating well on all sides. Shake off any excess. Add the chops to the pot and cook for 3 to 4 minutes, until well browned. Flip and cook another 3 to 4 minutes, until well browned. Spread the onion and garlic over the pork chops. Sprinkle the remaining ½ tsp salt, ¼ tsp pepper, and the basil over the onion and add the bay leaf. Top with the carrots.

In a medium bowl, mix together the broth, tomato sauce, and wine and pour over the carrots. With a fork, move the chops around to incorporate all of the other ingredients. Cover and bring to a simmer.

Bake for 1 hour and 45 minutes, or until the chops are very tender. Transfer the chops and carrots to a platter and cover to keep warm.

Place the pot over medium heat. Whisk together ¼ cup/ 60 ml water and the remaining 2 tbsp flour. Add to the pot and mix well. Cook for 5 minutes to thicken. Cut the chops in half to serve.

SLOW COOKER PORK CHOPS

The slow cooker is a mom's best friend. Just pile everything in there in the morning and a wonderful dinner appears in the evening. Pork chops, leeks, mushrooms, and potatoes create a full-belly warming meal with no hassle. I use a 6-qt/5.7-L slow cooker with low and high settings. Your mileage may vary. I don't serve this with anything additional because it's all in there.

1 tbsp salt

1 tsp black pepper

1 tsp granulated garlic

1 tsp granulated onion

1 tsp paprika

½ tsp dried thyme

6 boneless pork chops, about ½ in/12 mm thick

1 large leek, white and pale green parts only, washed, split, and sliced ½ in/12 mm thick

8 oz/225 g sliced baby portobella mushrooms

2 large Roma tomatoes, seeded and diced

2 russet potatoes, halved lengthwise and sliced about ½ in/12 mm thick

1 cup/240 ml vegetable broth

In a small bowl, combine the salt, pepper, granulated garlic, granulated onion, paprika, and thyme. Mix well. Using about one-third of the spice mixture, season the chops evenly on both sides.

Stand the chops up on their sides in the bottom of a 6-qt/5.7-L slow cooker. Top with the leek, then the mushrooms, and then the tomatoes, spreading each evenly. Sprinkle the vegetables with another third of the spice mixture. Lay the potato slices on top, pushing them lightly down into the vegetables. Sprinkle the top with the remaining spice mixture. Pour the broth over the top.

Put the lid on the slow cooker and turn it to high. Cook for about 8 hours, until the potatoes are very soft. Transfer the potatoes to a platter. Transfer the chops to the platter, being careful not to break them up. They will be very tender. Spoon the remaining sauce and vegetables over the top of the chops and potatoes before serving.

PORK CHOP PEPPER STEAK

A long time ago, I learned how to make pepper steak from Mrs. Rice, my friend Mike's mom. I've made it the same way for a long time. But now I've switched to pork chops and it's a great change. I can't say for sure that it's an improvement on Mrs. Rice's original, but I think she'd enjoy a plate of it—especially if you serve it with warm dinner rolls and some butter.

6 boneless pork chops, about ½ in/12 mm thick

¼ cup/30 g flour

½ tsp salt

½ tsp black pepper

¼ cup/60 ml vegetable oil

1 yellow onion, cut into medium dice

3 garlic cloves, crushed

One 28-oz/800-g can whole peeled tomatoes

1 cup/240 ml vegetable broth

2 tbsp soy sauce

2 green bell peppers, cut into ½-in/12-mm strips

Cooked white rice

Cut the pork chops into strips ½ by 2 in/12 mm by 5 cm. In a large bowl, combine the flour, salt, and pepper. Mix well. Heat the vegetable oil in a Dutch oven over medium-high heat. Dredge the pork chop strips in the flour mixture, coating well on all sides. Shake off any excess. Add the strips to the pan.

Cook for 7 to 8 minutes, stirring occasionally, until the pork strips are golden brown on all sides. Add the onion and garlic and mix well.

Pour the tomatoes and their juice into a large bowl and crush them with your hands. Add the tomatoes and juice to the pan. Mix well. Add the broth and soy sauce. Mix well.

Cover and bring to a simmer. Reduce the heat to maintain a simmer and cook for 20 minutes. Add the bell pepper strips and mix well. Return to a simmer and cook for 40 minutes more, until the meat and peppers are tender. (Check for salt and add if necessary.) Serve the mixture over the rice.

TATER TOT PORK CHOP CASSEROLE

My brother-in-law Dino knows how to make only one dish for dinner. If Dino is cooking dinner, the family is having Tater Tot Casserole. But his version doesn't have pork chops in it and this one does, so this recipe is for him. Dino is going to love it, and once he tries this he won't make that ground meat version ever again (I hope). Dino serves this all by itself, but I like to serve it with a side of steamed carrots.

6 boneless pork chops, about ½ in/12 mm thick

Salt

Black pepper

Paprika

1 tbsp vegetable oil

3 tbsp butter

½ red onion, finely chopped

8 oz/225 g sliced baby portobella mushrooms

2 garlic cloves, crushed

1 tbsp soy sauce

2 tbsp all-purpose flour

2 cups/480 ml milk

One 32-oz/910-g bag frozen Tater Tots

Preheat the oven to 350°F/180°C. Coat a 9-by-13-in/ 23-by-33-cm baking pan with vegetable spray. Season the pork chops on both sides with salt, pepper, and paprika. Heat a large skillet over medium-high heat. Add the vegetable oil and 1 tbsp of the butter. Stir until melted and blended. Add the chops to the skillet three at a time and cook for 3 to 4 minutes per side, until golden brown. Transfer the chops to the baking pan and arrange them in a single layer. Repeat for the second batch of chops, adding 1 tbsp butter.

When the last chops are out of the skillet, add the remaining 1 tbsp butter. When the butter is melted, add the onion and mix well. Cook for about 2 minutes, until they begin to soften. Add the mushrooms and garlic and mix well. Add the soy sauce, season with ½ tsp salt and ¼ tsp pepper, and mix well.

Cook for 7 to 8 minutes, stirring occasionally, until the mushrooms are soft. Add the flour and mix well. The mixture will tighten up, but that's normal. Continue stirring and cooking for 1 minute. Add the milk and mix well. Cook for 4 to 5 minutes, stirring occasionally, until the mixture comes to a simmer and everything is incorporated.

With a slotted spoon, spread the mushrooms over the chops evenly. Pour the sauce over all of the chops. Top with the Tater Tots, lining them up in a nice pattern. Bake for about 1 hour, until the mushroom mixture is bubbling and the tops of the Tater Tots are golden brown. Remove the casserole from the oven and let it rest for 5 minutes before serving.

CHEESY PORK CHOP SKILLET DINNER

Think of this as Pork Chop Helper, but a huge upgrade from the stuff in the box at the super-market. Using fresh ingredients, spices from your own cabinet, and pork chops makes this a healthier, tastier, and economical alternative to that store-bought version. Add a small chopped salad for a complete meal.

4 boneless pork chops, about ½ in/12 mm thick

1 tbsp all-purpose flour

Salt

Black pepper

4 tbsp/60 ml olive oil

3 cups/195 g dried rotini pasta

1 small onion, chopped

1 small green bell pepper, chopped

2 garlic cloves, crushed

One 14.5-oz/415-g can petite diced tomatoes

1 cup/240 ml vegetable broth

½ tsp dried oregano

½ tsp dried basil

2 cups/230 g shredded mild Cheddar cheese

Cut the pork chops into bite-size pieces. In a small bowl, mix together the flour, ½ tsp salt, and ½ tsp pepper. Sprinkle the flour mixture over the pork and toss to coat evenly. In a Dutch oven over medium-high heat, warm 2 tbsp of the olive oil. Add the meat and cook for 4 to 5 minutes, stirring occasionally, until golden brown. Remove the pork with a slotted spoon and set aside.

Meanwhile, cook the pasta per the box instructions to al dente. Drain well and set aside.

Add the remaining 2 tbsp oil to the hot pork pan. Add the onion, bell pepper, and garlic and stir well. Cook for about 4 minutes, until the onion is soft. Add the tomatoes with their juice and bring to a simmer. Add the broth, oregano, basil, ½ tsp salt, and ½ tsp pepper. Return to a simmer. Return the pork to the pot and return to a simmer. Cook for 10 minutes, until all the vegetables are soft and the broth has thickened. Add the cheese. Remove from the heat and mix until the cheese is fully incorporated. Add the cooked rotini and mix well. Check for salt and pepper and add, if desired, before serving.

PORK CHOPS AND DUMPLINGS

This is another classic one-pot dish that does very well with a switch to pork chops. After all, we know that pork chops taste better than that other stuff. The dumplings are the drop style that soak up the gravy and make a tasty complement to the pork chops. Buttered carrots on the side add flavor and color.

4 tbsp/90 ml vegetable oil

1 yellow onion, coarsely chopped

1 cup/130 g all-purpose flour

1 tbsp seasoned salt

6 boneless pork chops, about ¾ in/2 cm thick

2 cups/480 ml vegetable broth

½ tsp Worcestershire sauce

DUMPLINGS

¼ cup/60 ml vegetable oil

1 cup/240 ml milk

2½ cups/315 g all-purpose flour

1 tbsp baking powder

1 tsp salt

1 tsp black pepper

GRAVY

2 cups/480 ml beef broth

½ cup/55 g all-purpose flour

Heat 2 tbsp of the vegetable oil in a large deep skillet over medium heat. Add the onion and cook until slightly browned, about 10 minutes. Remove the onion from the pan and set aside. Add another 2 tbsp oil to the pan. On a flat plate, combine the flour and seasoned salt. Dredge the chops in the flour, coating well on all sides. Shake off any excess. Raise the heat to medium-high. Add the chops and cook for about 5 minutes, until golden brown. Flip the chops and cook for another 5 minutes, until golden brown. Add the reserved onion, the broth, and Worcestershire. Mix well. Cover and simmer for 20 minutes, until the chops begin to feel tender.

TO MAKE THE DUMPLINGS: In a medium bowl, whisk together the vegetable oil and milk just until blended. In a medium bowl, combine the flour, baking powder, salt, and pepper. Add the flour mixture to the oil-milk mixture and stir well until stiff. When the pork chops have cooked for 20 minutes, remove the cover and drop the dumpling mixture by tablespoonfuls on top of the chops and liquid. Cover the pan and simmer until the dumplings are cooked through, about 20 minutes. With a slotted spoon, transfer the dumplings to a platter. Transfer the chops to the platter and tent loosely with foil. Let them rest for 5 minutes.

TO MAKE THE GRAVY: Bring the drippings in the pan back to a simmer. In a medium bowl, whisk together the broth and flour. Add them to the drippings and mix well. Bring to a simmer and cook for about 5 minutes, until it reaches the desired thickness.

Serve the gravy over the chops and dumplings.

PORK CHOP
CHILI

In the world of competitive chili cooking, the only time you'd use pork is in the green chili contest, where the sauce is made with fresh green chiles and sometimes tomatillos. But in my world, there's no need to have restrictions like that. Pork chops and red chili powder combined with the usual chili suspects make a great dish. Top with shredded cheese and a few crackers on the side.

8 slices bacon

6 boneless pork chops, about ½ in/12 mm thick

Salt

Black pepper

1 large red onion, finely chopped

1 poblano chile, seeded and finely chopped

1 green bell pepper, finely chopped

1 jalapeño, seeded and finely chopped

3 garlic cloves, crushed

Two 10-oz/280-g cans diced tomatoes with green chiles

¼ cup/20 g good-quality chili powder

1 tbsp ground cumin

3 cups/720 ml vegetable broth

One 16-oz/455-g can dark red kidney beans, drained

2 tbsp flour (optional)

Preheat a Dutch oven over medium heat. Add the bacon and cook for 12 to 14 minutes, until crispy and well browned. Transfer it to a plate lined with paper towels to drain.

Raise the heat to medium-high. Season the pork chops liberally with salt and pepper. Place three of the chops in the pot. Cook for 3 to 4 minutes, until golden brown. Flip and cook for another 3 to 4 minutes, until golden brown. Transfer to a plate and repeat with the remaining chops. When all the chops are out of the pan, add the onion, poblano, bell pepper, jalapeño, and garlic. Mix well. Cook for about 5 minutes, stirring often, until the onion is soft. Add the tomatoes, chili powder, cumin, and 1 tsp salt. Mix well and cook for 1 minute to cook the spices. Add the broth and mix well. Bring it to a simmer. Chop the reserved bacon into small bits. Cut the pork chops into ½-in/12-mm pieces. Add the kidney beans, bacon, and pork chops to the pot. Mix well and return the chili to a simmer. Reduce the heat to maintain a low simmer.

Cook for 1 hour and 15 minutes, stirring occasionally, until the meat is tender. If you'd like it thicker, add ¼ cup/60 ml water mixed with the flour and stir well. Cook for 5 minutes more to thicken before serving.

PORK CHOP GUMBO

Gumbo is the dish that folks in Louisiana love to cook, discuss, sing about, and—most of all—eat. There seem to be no boundaries to what can be added to gumbo as long as you start with a roux and end with okra or filé to thicken the sauce. For me, pork chops and andouille sausage are a great combination and I prefer filé to okra for my thickener. Gumbo is always served with white rice and hot sauce on the side.

PORK STOCK

4 bone-in pork chops, about ¾ in/2 cm thick

Salt

Black pepper

2 tbsp vegetable oil

2 cups/480 ml chicken broth

2 carrots, peeled and coarsely chopped

2 celery stalks, coarsely chopped

1 medium onion, coarsely chopped

3 garlic cloves

1 jalapeño, seeded and coarsely chopped

2 bay leaves

ROUX

¾ cup/180 ml corn oil

¾ cup/90 g all-purpose flour

1 large red onion, cut into medium dice

3 celery stalks, cut into medium dice

2 green bell peppers, cut into medium dice

1 pound/455 g thinly sliced andouille or smoked pork sausage

3 garlic cloves, crushed

1 jalapeño, seeded and minced

One 15-oz/430-g can diced tomatoes

1 tbsp dried thyme

1½ tsp salt

1½ tsp black pepper

1 tbsp filé powder

TO MAKE THE STOCK: Season the pork chops with salt and pepper. Heat the vegetable oil in a Dutch oven over medium heat. Add two of the chops to the pot and cook for about 4 minutes, until golden brown. Flip the chops and cook for about 4 minutes more, until golden brown. Transfer the chops to a plate and repeat the process with the other two pork chops.

When all the chops are on the plate, pour the broth into the pan, scraping all the browned bits from the bottom. Add 1 qt/1 L water, the carrots, celery, onion, garlic, jalapeño, bay leaves, 1 tsp salt, and 1 tsp pepper. Mix well and bring to a simmer.

Cover and cook for 1 hour, stirring occasionally but being careful not to break up the pork chops. Remove from the heat and let the stock rest for 30 minutes. Remove the chops, being careful not to break them up. Cover the chops with plastic wrap and set aside. Strain the stock through a colander and discard the vegetables, or have them for lunch. Measure out 6 cups/1.4 L of the stock and refrigerate any extra for another use.

TO MAKE THE ROUX: Preheat a clean large Dutch oven over medium-low heat. Add the corn oil and flour and mix well with a wooden spoon.

Cook the roux, stirring constantly, until it reaches a dark brown chocolate color. This will take at least 20 minutes and up to 45 and can't be rushed. Be very careful not to burn the roux or you'll need to start all over. Turn the heat down if you feel it's close to burning. This is particularly high risk toward the end.

As soon as you think the roux is dark enough, or your nerve runs out, add the onion, celery, and bell peppers and continue stirring. This will cool the roux and end the risk of it burning. Cook and stir for 5 minutes more, until the vegetables get soft. Add the sausage, garlic, and jalapeño. Continue cooking and stirring for another 5 minutes. Add the tomatoes with their juice. Return to a simmer and cook another 5 minutes. Add the 6 cups/1.4 L pork stock, thyme, salt, and pepper.

Bring to a simmer, cover, and cook for 1 hour, stirring occasionally. Remove the pork chop meat from the bones, discarding the bones and fat. Break the meat into bite-size pieces and add it to the gumbo. Return to a simmer. Cover the pot and cook, stirring occasionally, for 30 minutes. Uncover and continue cooking, stirring occasionally, for 30 minutes. Add the filé powder and mix well. Cook for 15 minutes, stirring occasionally, until thickened before serving.

PORK CHOP NOODLE SOUP

I believe that pork chop noodle soup cures colds better than any other. Once you try using bone-in pork chops in your soup, you will become a convert. For this recipe, I would recommend making homemade pork stock for an even richer soup. I often serve this soup with grilled Swiss cheese sandwiches.

3 bone-in pork chops, about ¾ in/2 cm thick

Salt

Black pepper

2 tbsp vegetable oil

2 cups/480 ml chicken broth or Pork Stock (page 20)

4 cups/960 ml unsalted vegetable broth

1 red onion, chopped

2 large celery stalks, chopped

4 carrots, chopped

2 garlic cloves, crushed

1 tsp dried thyme

½ tsp dried basil

1 cup/65 g dried rotini pasta

Season the pork chops with salt and pepper. Heat the vegetable oil in a Dutch oven over medium-high heat. Add the chops and cook for about 4 minutes, until golden brown. Flip and cook for 4 minutes more, until golden brown. Transfer the chops to a plate and set aside.

Pour half of the chicken broth into the pot, scraping all the browned bits from the bottom. Add the remaining chicken broth, vegetable broth, onion, celery, carrots, and garlic. Mix well and bring to a simmer. Add 1 qt/1 L water, the thyme, basil, 2 tsp salt, and 1 tsp pepper. Mix well and bring to a simmer. Add the chops back to the pot and return to a simmer. Reduce the heat and simmer for 90 minutes, stirring occasionally, being careful not to break up the chops.

Transfer the chops to a plate, trying not to break them up. Set aside to cool. Raise the heat and bring the soup to a boil. Add the pasta and cook for about 12 minutes, until tender. When the chops are cool, pull them apart, discarding all the bones and fat. For a rustic look, break the meat up with your hands or, for a more refined look, use your knife to dice it. Add the meat back to the soup and stir well. Taste for salt and pepper, and add if needed, before serving.

PORK CHOP, LEEK, AND POTATO SOUP

SERVES ABOUT 10

This is a classic soup with the decadent addition of pork chops taking it over the top. The leeks and chops come together to make an amazing broth that's perfect for tailgating or any time you need something to warm you inside and out. This begs to be served with a hunk of crusty French bread for dipping.

3 bone-in pork chops, ¾ in/2 cm thick

Salt

Black pepper

3 slices bacon

2 large leeks, split, washed, white and most of the green parts sliced

2 large celery stalks, cut into medium dice

2 garlic cloves, crushed

2 large russet potatoes, peeled and cut into medium dice

1 qt/1 L unsalted vegetable broth

1 tsp dried thyme

1 tsp dried basil

½ cup/120 ml milk

Season the pork chops with salt and pepper and set aside. Heat a large Dutch oven over medium heat. Add the bacon and cook until crispy, 6 to 7 minutes. Transfer the bacon to a plate lined with paper towels and set aside. Add the pork chops to the pot and cook for 4 to 5 minutes, until golden brown. Flip the chops and cook for 4 to 5 minutes more, until golden brown. Transfer the chops to another plate and set aside.

Add the leeks, celery, and garlic to the pot. Mix well and cook for 5 minutes, stirring occasionally, until the leeks have softened. Add the potatoes and mix well. Cook for 3 to 4 minutes, stirring occasionally, until the potatoes are incorporated. Add the broth, 1 cup/240 ml water, the thyme and basil and mix well. Season with 2 tsp salt and 1 tsp pepper. Chop the reserved bacon and add it to the pot. Bring to a simmer. Lay the reserved pork chops on top of the soup. Cover and simmer for 1 hour and 15 minutes, until the chops are tender, stirring occasionally but being careful not to break up the chops.

Transfer the chops to a plate to cool, being careful not to leave any bones behind. Add the milk to the soup and stir well. Taste for salt and add if needed. When the chops are cool enough to handle, break them into small pieces and discard the bones. Return the pork chop meat to the pot and mix well before serving.

RAY'S SPECIAL OVEN CHOPS

Some days you just feel like doing a crazy kitchen experiment, and that's how this recipe came to be. I looked around the pantry and what did I see? Mayo, barbecue sauce, and panko, and there's always bacon in the fridge at my house. I used all of them to create these delicious chops, proving that necessity is indeed the mother of invention. These are best served with a simple side salad.

4 bone-in pork chops, about ½ in/12 mm thick

Salt

Black pepper

⅓ cup/70 g mayonnaise

1 cup/115 g panko or bread crumbs

1 tsp paprika

¼ cup/60 ml barbecue sauce

4 slices bacon, cooked and crumbled

1½ cups/175 g finely shredded Cheddar cheese

Preheat the oven to 375°F/190°C. Coat a medium baking sheet with vegetable spray. Season the chops with salt and pepper on both sides. Smear the mayonnaise on all sides of the chops.

On a flat plate, combine the panko, 1 tsp salt, 1 tsp pepper, and the paprika. Dredge the chops in the panko mixture, coating well on all sides. Set them on the baking sheet.

Bake for 15 minutes. Gently spread the barbecue sauce evenly over the chops. Top each chop with one-fourth of the bacon and one-fourth of the cheese. Bake for 15 minutes more, until the cheese is melted. Transfer the chops to a platter and let them rest for 5 minutes before serving.

PORK CHOPS AND WHITE BEANS

Nothing warms your soul like a kettle full of creamy white beans. I like mine with a lot of big flavor, so I add a good amount of aromatics, spicy sausage, and pork chops. The consistency will change as they cook, so don't worry if the mixture seems thin. It will continue to thicken even after it's done cooking. Besides, a little fresh cornbread on the side will soak up any of the rich gravy.

1 lb/455 g dry great Northern beans

½ cup/120 ml vegetable oil, plus more as needed

6 bone-in pork chops, about ¾ in/2 cm thick

Salt

Black pepper

½ cup/55 g all-purpose flour

1 red onion, finely diced

3 celery stalks, finely diced

1 large green bell pepper, finely diced

4 garlic cloves, crushed

1 lb/455 g diced andouille sausage

1 tbsp tomato paste

2 tsp dried thyme

1 qt/1 L vegetable broth

The night before you plan to cook, place the beans in a large nonreactive bowl. Pick through the beans to remove and discard any small stones or debris. Add water to cover the beans by at least 2 in/5 cm. Cover the bowl and let soak overnight at room temperature. Drain the beans and set aside.

In a large heavy Dutch oven over medium-high heat, warm ¼ cup/60 ml of the vegetable oil. Season the chops with salt and pepper. Place the flour on a flat plate and dredge the chops in the flour, coating well on all sides. Shake off any excess. Fry three chops at a time until golden brown, about 5 minutes per side, adding extra oil as needed. Transfer the chops to a platter lined with paper towels to drain. Cover with aluminum foil and set aside.

Add the remaining ¼ cup/60 ml oil to the pot. Add the onion, celery, and bell pepper and mix well. Cook for 3 to 4 minutes, until the onion is opaque. Add the garlic and sausage and mix well. Cook for 4 to 5 minutes, until the bell pepper and celery are soft. Add the tomato paste, 1 tbsp salt, 1 tsp pepper, and the thyme and mix well. Cook for 2 to 3 minutes, until the tomato paste is incorporated. Add the broth and 1 qt/1 L water and bring to a simmer. Add the beans and mix well. Cover and simmer for 1 hour, stirring occasionally. Add the pork chops and mix well. Return to a simmer. Cover and simmer for 1 hour more, stirring occasionally and being careful not to break up the pork chops. Remove the cover and cook for 45 minutes more, stirring occasionally and being careful not to break up the pork chops. Cook until the beans are soft and the gravy is the consistency of a bowl of chili. Transfer the chops to a platter and the beans to a bowl to serve.

CHAPTER 5
International Pork Chops

We are lucky as cooks to have access to interesting culinary ideas and ingredients from many cultures well beyond our own. Some of the dishes we enjoy these days are very authentic and others are sort of a hybrid, taking an authentic ethnic dish and transforming it into something that others will enjoy even if they didn't grow up eating it. Many have become adopted dishes that we eat and prepare regularly regardless of our heritage or cultural connection to them. Good is good and there are no boundaries. Many of the dishes in this chapter could even be considered in the same class as the classics in chapter 2, with an international spin of course. But these dishes all have one thing in common: None was originally made with pork chops. Well, not until I got hold of them anyway. As usual, pork chops make a tasty and tender substitute, often giving the old dish a fresh and new taste. Pork chops match well with just about any flavor combination, and here they are paired with Spanish, Asian, Italian, Creole, and other flavors with great success. And if a beloved dish isn't listed here, just buy some pork chops and plug them into your favorite international recipe. I think it will work out very well.

PORK CHOP SUEY

SERVES 4

To most Americans, chop suey is the original stir-fry and we love it. This simple version uses pork chops and bok choy. There are some noodles used as an ingredient, but I still serve this over white rice.

2 oz/55 g dried lo mein noodles, broken in half

4 bone-in pork chops, about ¾ in/2 cm thick

Salt

Black pepper

Paprika

3 tbsp olive oil

¼ cup/60 ml beef broth

½ cup/60 g diced celery

1 cup/125 g diced bok choy stalks, plus
1 cup/65 g coarsely chopped bok choy leaves

1 red onion, halved and thinly sliced

1 red or orange bell pepper, cut into thin strips

1 tsp minced fresh ginger

2 garlic cloves, minced

½ cup/120 ml soy sauce

¼ cup/60 ml orange juice

¼ cup/60 ml hoisin sauce

1 tbsp brown sugar

1 tsp cornstarch

½ cup/80 g sliced water chestnuts

4 scallions, thinly sliced on the diagonal

Cook the lo mein as instructed on the package. Drain and set aside.

Season the pork chops with salt, pepper, and paprika on both sides. Heat the olive oil in a large skillet over medium-high heat. Add the chops and cook for 3 to 4 minutes, until golden brown. Flip the chops and cook for 3 to 4 minutes more, until golden brown. Add the broth. Bring to a simmer. Reduce the heat, cover, and simmer for about 5 minutes to cook the chops through. Transfer the chops to a plate and set aside.

Raise the temperature to medium-high. Add the celery, bok choy stalks, onion, and bell pepper. Mix well. Cook for about 5 minutes, until the onion is soft. Add the ginger and garlic and mix well. In a medium bowl, combine the soy sauce, orange juice, hoisin sauce, brown sugar, and cornstarch. Mix well and add to the skillet. Cook for 5 minutes, until all the vegetables are soft. Add the noodles, bok choy leaves, and water chestnuts. Mix well and cook for 3 to 4 minutes to thicken. (If the mixture is too thick, add a little more broth.) Add the pork chops, pushing them down into the sauce. Cover and cook 3 to 4 minutes more, until the pork chops are heated through. To serve, divide the vegetable-noodle mixture evenly among four plates and top each with a pork chop. Garnish the top with the scallions.

THAI PORK CHOPS IN BANANA LEAVES

Thai cuisine embraces a lot of fish and vegetables, but the flavors are very well suited to tasty and tender pork chops. If you like it spicy, just add a little more of the red chili flakes. The sauce is delicious with white rice.

4 boneless pork chops, about ¾ in/2 cm thick

Salt

Black pepper

¼ cup/20 g chopped fresh cilantro

3 scallions, white and green parts thinly sliced

2 garlic cloves, crushed

1 tbsp minced fresh ginger

½ lime, juiced

1 tbsp peanut oil

1 tsp soy sauce

½ tsp fish sauce

¼ tsp red chili flakes

4 banana leaf pieces, about 8 in/20 cm square, softened (available at Asian markets)

SAUCE

One 14-oz/400-g can coconut milk

1 tbsp cornstarch

1 tbsp Thai chili sauce

1 tbsp finely chopped fresh cilantro

½ tsp salt

Preheat the oven to 350°F/180°C. Season the pork chops with salt and pepper, then set aside. In a small bowl, combine the cilantro, scallions, garlic, ginger, lime juice, peanut oil, soy sauce, fish sauce, chili flakes, and ¼ tsp salt. Mix well. Lay a pork chop in the center of each banana leaf piece. Top each chop with one-fourth of the garlic mixture. Fold up the sides over each chop and then fold up the ends, forming a square package. Tie each snugly with a piece of butcher string in each direction. Place the packages on a baking sheet. Bake for 30 minutes.

TO MAKE THE SAUCE: Pour the coconut milk into a small saucepan over medium heat. Add the cornstarch and whisk to blend. Bring it to a simmer. Reduce the heat to maintain a simmer and cook for 12 to 14 minutes, stirring occasionally, until the milk is reduced by half. Add the chili sauce, cilantro, and salt. Mix well and keep warm off the heat.

When the pork chops are done, transfer each package to a serving plate. Cut the string and discard. Open the leaves and top each pork chop with a couple teaspoons of the sauce. Serve with the remaining sauce on the side.

SPICY GRILLED JERK PORK CHOPS

Jerk is the classic Jamaican spice for grilling and it's a big bold smoking-hot taste. I've used three chiles for this to create a medium heat level by jerk standards. Add or subtract to taste, but remember: If it's not hot, it's not jerk. Always wear food-service gloves when handling chiles because they can hurt if you get some under a nail or touch your eye. The classic sides to serve with this are rice and beans.

JERK PASTE

1 large onion, coarsely chopped

12 to 16 scallions, white and some green parts coarsely chopped

10 garlic cloves, coarsely chopped

3 Scotch bonnet chiles (or habaneros), seeds and veins removed and coarsely chopped

¼ cup/25 g ground allspice

3 tbsp salt

1 tbsp smoked paprika

1 tsp ground cinnamon

1 tsp ground nutmeg

1 tsp ground dried thyme

¼ cup/60 ml soy sauce

¼ cup/60 ml vegetable oil

¼ cup/60 ml white vinegar

6 bone-in pork chops, about ¾ in/2 cm thick

TO MAKE THE JERK PASTE: Place the onion, scallions, garlic, and chiles in the bowl of a large food processor fitted with the metal blade. Top with the allspice, salt, paprika, cinnamon, nutmeg, and thyme. Pour in the soy sauce, vegetable oil, vinegar, and ¼ cup/60 ml water. Pulse to break everything down and then process for about 30 seconds, until all the big chunks are gone. Put the jerk paste in a big nonreactive bowl.

One at a time, dredge the pork chops in the paste, leaving them in the bowl when fully covered. Cover the bowl and refrigerate for at least 1 hour and up to 8 hours.

Prepare an outdoor grill to cook direct over medium heat. Using cooking gloves to handle the pork, pull each chop out of the paste and place it directly on the grill grate, keeping as much paste on the chop as possible. Discard the remaining paste. Cook for 4 to 5 minutes per side, until the chops are golden brown and have reached an internal temperature of 150°F/65°C. Transfer them to a platter and tent loosely with aluminum foil. Let them rest for 5 minutes before serving.

MOJO-MARINATED PORK CHOPS

Mojo is the classic Caribbean marinade that relies heavily on sour orange juice. It's really a unique flavor, so try to find the juice or order it online for the authentic taste. Otherwise, substitute regular orange juice with lime juice added. Typically, this marinade goes on pork roasts and requires a couple days of marinating, but it works just as well on a quick-marinated pork chop. I like to serve this with black beans and white rice.

MOJO SAUCE

1¼ cups/300 ml sour orange juice (or 1 cup/240 ml orange juice and ¼ cup/60 ml lime juice)

2 tbsp olive oil

6 garlic cloves, crushed

1 tbsp salt

1 tsp black pepper

1 tsp onion powder

1 tsp ground cumin

1 tsp dried oregano

4 bone-in pork chops, about ¾ in/2 cm thick

TO MAKE THE MOJO SAUCE: At least 12 hours before you plan to cook, in a medium bowl, combine the sour orange juice, olive oil, garlic, salt, pepper, onion powder, cumin, and oregano. Mix well.

Place the pork chops in a large zip-top bag. Pour the mixture over the chops and seal the bag, squeezing out as much air as possible. Refrigerate for at least 12 hours and up to 24 hours.

Prepare an outdoor grill to cook direct over medium-high heat. Remove the chops from the marinade and pat them dry with a paper towel. Place them on the grill and cook for 3 to 4 minutes, until golden brown. Flip the chops and cook for 3 to 4 minutes more, until golden brown and cooked to an internal temperature of 150°F/65°C. Transfer the chops to a plate to let rest for 5 minutes before serving.

ARROZ CON PUERCO CHOPS

SERVES 4

That wonderful classic dish of saffron rice goes very well with pork chops stepping in as the headliner. The original dish comes from Spain and is popular throughout South America and the Caribbean, so it's no surprise that you see it often in the restaurants around Tampa's Ybor City, very near to the place I call home. A simple side salad completes the meal.

Small pinch of saffron

4 boneless pork chops, about ¾ in/2 cm thick

Seasoned salt

Black pepper

¼ cup/60 ml olive oil

½ red onion, finely diced

½ green bell pepper, finely diced

6 garlic cloves, crushed

1 cup/240 ml chicken broth

1½ tsp salt

1 cup/180 g converted rice

1 tbsp diced pimientos

Preheat the oven to 350°F/180°C. Place the saffron on a small piece of aluminum foil and toast it in the oven for 4 minutes. Remove and set aside.

Season the chops liberally with seasoned salt and pepper. Heat the olive oil in a heavy Dutch oven over medium-high heat. Add the chops and cook for 3 to 4 minutes, until golden brown. Flip the chops and cook for 3 to 4 minutes more, until golden brown. Transfer the chops to a plate and set aside.

Add the onion, bell pepper, and garlic to the pot. Cook, stirring occasionally, for 3 to 4 minutes, until the onion is soft. Add the broth, 1 cup/240 ml water, the salt, 1 tsp pepper, and the saffron. Mix well and bring to a boil. Add the rice and mix well. Return it to a boil. Remove from the heat. Mix the rice well and return the chops to the pot. Cover and put the pot in the oven to bake for 30 minutes. Remove from the oven and let rest for 5 minutes before uncovering. Transfer the pork chops to a plate. Add the pimientos to the rice and mix them in, fluffing all of the rice. Return the chops to the pot and serve it family-style.

SANGRITA PORK CHOPS

SERVES 4

The inspiration for this recipe comes from my friend Chef Sue Torres. Sue and I are kindred spirits in the kitchen and we love to cook and eat together. Her idea was to make *sangrita* to season the chops before grilling. *Sangrita* is a traditional juice and chile chaser to be sipped with tequila in Mexico. It's spicy, with a good hit of citrus, and complements pork chops nicely. Serve these with black beans, white rice, and a shot of tequila (naturally).

SANGRITA

3 large beefsteak tomatoes, cut into quarters

¼ large white onion

2 garlic cloves, unpeeled

1 serrano chile, stem removed

2 tbsp chipotle purée (see Note)

1 orange, juiced

1 lemon, juiced

½ tsp salt

½ tsp black pepper

6 bone-in pork chops, about ¾ in/2 cm thick

TO MAKE THE SANGRITA: Preheat the oven to 350°F/180°C. Place the tomatoes, onion, garlic, and serrano on a baking sheet. Roast them for 30 minutes. Transfer the garlic and serrano to a plate and set aside. Roast the tomatoes and onion another 45 minutes, until the onion is soft. Remove from the oven. Lift the skins off the tomatoes and discard. Remove the peels from the garlic. Put the tomatoes, onion, garlic, serrano, chipotle purée, orange juice, lemon juice, salt, and pepper in a blender. Blend on high for 30 seconds, until smooth. Transfer to a medium bowl and cover. Let cool for about 30 minutes.

Prepare an outdoor grill to cook direct over medium heat. Reserve ½ cup/120 ml of the sangrita to use as a sauce. Dunk the chops in the remaining sangrita and place them on the grill. Cook for about 10 minutes, flipping often and spooning additional sauce over the chops each time you flip. When the chops are golden brown and have reached an internal temperature of 150°F/65°C, transfer them to a platter to rest for 5 minutes. Discard the sangrita mix that you've been basting with. Serve the chops with the reserved sangrita as a sauce on the side.

NOTE: CHIPOTLE PURÉE
Place the contents of one 7-oz/200-g can of chipotles in adobo sauce in a blender. Rinse out the can with ¼ cup/60 ml water and pour it into the blender. Add a pinch of salt and blend until smooth. This will keep covered in the refrigerator for 1 month.

P.93

PORK CHOP GUACADILLAS

I call these "guacadillas" instead of quesadillas because of the avocado and other guacamole-friendly ingredients inside. You can cook these on the outdoor grill for a little extra smoky flavor or even cook them ahead to eat at room temperature for tailgating. All you need with these are homemade salsa, sour cream, and sliced jalapeños.

3 boneless pork chops, about ¾ in/2 cm thick

Salt

Black pepper

Chili powder

1 ripe avocado, peeled and pitted

½ cup/115 g cream cheese, at room temperature

2 medium Roma tomatoes, seeded and chopped

¼ cup/35 g canned chopped green chiles (such as New Mexico or poblano)

¼ cup/30 g finely chopped red onion

¼ cup/20 g chopped fresh cilantro

½ lime, zested

Eight 10-in/25-cm flour tortillas

2 cups/240 g finely shredded mixed Jack and Cheddar cheeses

Preheat the broiler on high. Season the pork chops with salt, pepper, and chili powder. Place the chops on a broiler pan or baking sheet and cook for 5 to 6 minutes, until golden brown. Flip and cook for 5 to 6 minutes more, until they reach an internal temperature of 150°F/ 65°C. Transfer them to a plate to cool.

In a medium bowl, smash the avocado with a fork. Add the cream cheese and mix well. Add the tomatoes, chiles, onion, cilantro, lime zest, ¼ tsp salt, and ¼ tsp pepper. Mix well until blended. Lay four of the tortillas on a flat surface. Top each with one-fourth of the avocado mixture and spread it evenly over the whole surface. Thinly slice the pork chops. Spread the slices evenly over the avocado mixture. Top each tortilla with ½ cup/60 g of the cheese and spread evenly. Top each with another tortilla and press lightly to combine the ingredients.

Preheat a large nonstick skillet over medium heat. Place an assembled guacadilla in the pan. Cook for 2 to 3 minutes, until golden brown. Gently flip. Cook for 2 to 3 minutes more, until golden brown and the cheeses are melted. Transfer to a cutting board and repeat until all the guacadillas are cooked. Slice the guacadillas into six wedges each to serve.

PORK CHOP CARNITAS

The translation of *carnitas* is literally "little meats," but on the plate the flavor is big and bold. Carnitas are the common pork offering at Mexican restaurants in the United States and are typically made with the fattier cuts like Boston butt or the picnic ham. Making them with pork chops lightens things up but keeps that great pork flavor to stand up to the spices. Traditional sides include tortillas, rice, and refried beans and that's the way I like to eat this.

4 boneless pork chops, about 1 in/2.5 cm thick

Salt

Black pepper

1 cup/240 ml chicken broth

1 small onion, chopped

1 orange, juiced

1 lime, juiced

2 garlic cloves, crushed

1 jalapeño, seeded and ribs removed, finely chopped

1 tsp dried oregano

1 tsp ground cumin

1 tsp chili powder

1 tbsp olive oil

Season the pork chops with salt and pepper and set aside. In a medium bowl, combine the broth, onion, orange juice, lime juice, garlic, jalapeño, oregano, cumin, chili powder, ½ tsp salt, and ½ tsp pepper. Mix well. Heat the olive oil in a large skillet over medium-high heat. Add the chops and cook for about 4 minutes, until golden brown. Flip the chops and cook another 3 to 4 minutes, until golden brown. Pour the orange juice mixture over the chops. Bring to a simmer. Cover and cook for 30 minutes. Flip the chops and continue cooking for another 30 minutes, until the pork is tender. Transfer the chops to a baking sheet.

Preheat the broiler on high. Strain the sauce and return it to the pan. Continue simmering it until reduced to ½ cup/120 ml. Transfer the sauce to a bowl. Break the pork chops into bite-size pieces. Brush them with the reduced liquid. Place them under the broiler for 4 to 5 minutes, until well browned. Remove from the broiler and transfer to a plate. Serve with the remaining sauce on the side for topping the carnitas.

PORK CHOP ÉTOUFFÉE

Étouffée is a French word that literally means "smothered," and is a Cajun creation served throughout south Louisiana. It's typically made with shellfish, but when you look at the ingredients, they actually pair beautifully with pork chops. No need to add anything to this meal except hot sauce.

4 boneless pork chops, about ¾ in/2 cm thick

Salt

Black pepper

2 tbsp vegetable oil

¼ cup/55 g butter

2 tbsp all-purpose flour

½ red onion, finely chopped

1 large celery stalk, finely chopped

½ green bell pepper, finely chopped

1½ cups/360 ml vegetable broth

2 large Roma tomatoes, seeded and diced

3 garlic cloves, crushed

1 bay leaf

½ tsp dried thyme

¼ tsp cayenne pepper

3 cups/450 g cooked long-grain white rice

Season the pork chops with salt and pepper on both sides. Heat the vegetable oil in a Dutch oven over medium heat. Add the chops and cook for 3 to 4 minutes, until golden brown. Flip the chops and cook for 3 to 4 minutes more, until golden brown. Transfer the chops to a plate and set aside.

Add the butter to the pot and stir to melt. Add the flour and mix well. Continue mixing and scraping the bottom until the mixture turns the color of peanut butter, about 2 minutes. Add the onion, celery, and bell pepper and cook, stirring often, until the vegetables begin to soften, about 2 minutes. Deglaze the pan by adding the broth and scraping the bottom of the pan as it cooks. Add the tomatoes, garlic, bay leaf, 1 tsp salt, ¼ tsp pepper, the thyme, and cayenne. Mix well and bring to a simmer. Add the chops and return to a simmer. Cover and reduce the heat to maintain a simmer. Cook for 45 minutes, stirring occasionally.

Uncover the chops and cook another 15 minutes to thicken the sauce. Put one-fourth of the rice on each of four plates. Top with a pork chop and enough of the gravy to smother it all to serve.

PORK CHOPS CORDON BLEU

Cordon bleu translates from the French as "blue ribbon," and there is a very fancy cooking school that uses the name. But the original dish is an American creation of chicken with ham and Swiss cheese as the stuffing. For my pork chop version, I did things a little differently by using the stuffing as a topping and in the process created a very fun new approach to the concept. I usually make some rice pilaf and buttered carrots to go with this recipe.

¼ cup/30 g all-purpose flour

½ tsp salt

½ tsp black pepper

1 egg

½ cup/30 g fresh bread crumbs

1 tsp paprika

¼ cup/60 ml vegetable oil

4 boneless pork chops, about ¾ in/2 cm thick

4 oz/115 g thickly sliced good-quality ham, cut into small dice

1 cup/115 g grated Swiss cheese

On a flat plate, mix together the flour, salt, and pepper. In a shallow bowl, whisk the egg with 1 tbsp water until well blended. On another flat plate, mix the bread crumbs with the paprika. Heat the oil in a large skillet over medium heat. Dredge a chop in the flour mixture, covering all sides. Shake off any excess. Dip it in the egg mixture, shaking off any excess. Dredge it in the bread-crumb mixture, covering all sides. Shake off any excess bread crumbs. Set the chop on a platter and repeat with the others. Put the chops in the skillet and cook for about 5 minutes, until golden brown. Flip the chops and cook for another 4 to 5 minutes, until golden brown and they reach an internal temperature of 150°F/65°C. Transfer the chops to a baking sheet.

Preheat the broiler to high. In a small bowl, mix together the ham and cheese. Place one-fourth of the ham mixture on top of each of the chops. Broil them for 4 to 5 minutes, until the cheese is melted and lightly browned. Transfer to a plate and let rest for 5 minutes before serving.

PORK CHOPS SALTIMBOCCA

SERVES 4

Saltimbocca is an Italian dish that features thin slices of meat topped with prosciutto and sage. It's typically rolled and sautéed and served with a pan sauce made with butter and white wine. It's a simple combination that works beautifully with thinly sliced pork chops. There won't be enough sauce to cover a side of pasta, so I serve this with angel hair pasta tossed with a little bit of garlic, olive oil, and Parmesan cheese. The photo shows the prosciutto rolled on the outside, but I like it on the inside, which is more traditional.

8 boneless pork chops, about ¼ in/6 mm thick

Salt

Black pepper

12 large fresh sage leaves

8 thin slices prosciutto

½ cup/55 g all-purpose flour

2 tbsp olive oil

4 tbsp/55 g butter

2 cups/480 ml dry white wine

2 garlic cloves, crushed

With a heavy meat mallet, pound the chops until they are very thin and about the size of a saucer. Season the tops lightly with salt and pepper. Lay a slice of prosciutto on top of each chop, folding the end under if necessary. Lay a sage leaf across the middle of each slice of prosciutto. Roll the chops up around the prosciutto and tie each with a piece of butcher string.

Chop the remaining sage and set aside. Combine the flour, ½ tsp salt, and ¼ tsp pepper on a flat plate. Roll the chops in the flour to coat evenly. Shake off the excess.

Heat a large heavy skillet over medium-high heat. Add the olive oil and 2 tbsp of the butter and heat until the butter is melted and bubbling, swirling to combine. Add the pork chops and cook, turning occasionally, for about 8 minutes, until golden brown on all sides and cooked through. Transfer the chops to a serving plate and cover loosely with aluminum foil.

Add the remaining 2 tbsp butter to the pan and cook until melted and lightly browned. Deglaze the pan by pouring in the wine and mixing well, scraping up all the browned bits from the bottom of the pan. Add the garlic and reserved sage. Cook the sauce, stirring occasionally, until reduced by half, about 3 minutes. Pour the sauce over the chops to serve.

PORK CHOPS PARMIGIANA

This is the classic Italian restaurant red-sauce dish, but it gets new life when pork chops join the party. Add fresh garlic bread and a side salad.

SAUCE

¼ cup/60 ml olive oil

1 cup/125 g finely chopped onion

4 garlic cloves, crushed

One 28-oz/800-g can crushed tomatoes

2 tbsp chopped fresh basil

1 tsp dried oregano

½ tsp salt

½ tsp black pepper

½ cup/55 g all-purpose flour

½ tsp salt

½ tsp black pepper

2 eggs

1 cup/115 g dried bread crumbs

¼ cup/30 ml olive oil

6 boneless pork chops, about ½ in/12 mm thick

3 cups/350 g shredded mozzarella cheese

1 cup/115 g grated Parmesan cheese

Preheat the oven to 400°F/200°C.

TO MAKE THE SAUCE: Place a 3-qt/2.8-L saucepan over medium-high heat and add the olive oil. When the oil is hot, add the onion and cook, stirring occasionally, for 3 minutes. Add the garlic and cook, stirring occasionally, for 2 minutes, until the onion is soft. Add the tomatoes and bring to a simmer. Add the basil, oregano, salt, pepper, and ½ cup/120 ml water. Return to a simmer, then reduce the heat and cover. Simmer for 20 minutes.

Meanwhile, combine the flour, salt, and pepper on a flat plate and mix well. In a shallow bowl, beat the eggs lightly with 1 tbsp water. Place the bread crumbs on a flat plate. Heat the olive oil in a large skillet over medium-high heat. Dredge a chop in the flour, covering all sides. Shake off any excess. Dip it in the egg mixture, shaking off any excess. Dredge it in the bread-crumb mixture, covering all sides. Shake off any excess bread crumbs. Set the chop on a platter and repeat with the others. Place the chops in the skillet and cook for 2 to 3 minutes per side, until golden brown. Do this in two batches if necessary. (The chops will finish cooking in the oven.) Transfer the chops to a plate covered with paper towels to drain.

Spread half of the sauce on the bottom of a 9-by-13-in/23-by-33-cm baking pan. Lay the chops on top of the sauce, cover with the remaining sauce, and top with the cheeses. Bake for about 30 minutes, until the sauce is bubbly and the cheese is golden brown. Remove from the oven and let rest for 10 minutes before serving.

IT'S A CANADIAN PORK CHOP, EH!

This recipe comes from my Canadian buddy, Chef Ted Reader (he took the photo on the next page, too). I get to work with a lot of talented chefs, but Teddy is in a league of his own when it comes to creative cooking. He calls these Canadian pork chops with an Italian twist. Ted tells me that Toronto has the largest Italian community in the world outside of Italy, so it's no surprise that he's been influenced by their food. Chef Ted suggests serving these with pasta and fresh marinara.

THE WINE BRINE

One 750-ml bottle dry white wine, chilled

1 cup/240 ml white grape juice, chilled

6 garlic cloves, sliced

4 sprigs fresh oregano

½ tsp black peppercorns

¼ tsp red chili flakes

⅓ cup/95 g non-iodized table salt

½ cup/120 ml boiling water

6 bone-in pork chops, about 1½ in/4 cm thick

THE MEAT-A-BALL STUFFING

Six ½-oz/14-g balls fresh mozzarella cheese

2 slices crusty Italian bread, about 1 by 4 in/ 2.5 by 10 cm

¼ cup/60 ml whole milk

4 links coarse-ground sweet or hot Italian sausage

⅓ cup/45 g finely diced white onion

3 garlic cloves, minced

1 tbsp chopped fresh oregano

Kosher salt

Black pepper

Olive oil

Splash of white wine

Pinch of chili flakes

2 red oak cooking planks, about 12 by 8 by ½ in/ 30.5 cm by 20 cm by 12 mm

TO MAKE THE BRINE: Reserve a splash of the wine for the stuffing. In a large nonreactive pot or bucket, combine the wine, grape juice, 6 cups/1.4 L cold water, the garlic, oregano sprigs, peppercorns, and chili flakes. Stir. Put the salt in a small bowl and add the boiling water. Stir to dissolve. Pour the salt-water mixture into the brine; stir and set aside.

continued P.103

Place the pork chops in the brine, making sure they are completely submerged. Cover and refrigerate for 12 to 18 hours.

TO MAKE THE STUFFING: Put the mozzarella balls on a plate, making sure they don't touch, and freeze them for about 15 minutes. Tear the bread slices into uniform chunks, about ¾ in/2 cm square, and place them in a medium bowl. Pour the milk over the bread and gently mix to ensure that all of the bread is wet from the milk. Let stand for 10 minutes. Remove the sausage from the casings, discarding the casings. Put the meat in a large bowl. Add the onion, garlic, oregano, ½ tsp salt, and ½ tsp pepper. Drain the milk from the bread, squeezing out as much milk as possible. Add the bread to the sausage mixture. Add a splash of olive oil and the splash of wine and season with the chili flakes. Gently mix. Remove the cheese from the freezer. Form the meat into six uniform-size balls, packing the meat loosely, and stuffing each sausage meat-a-ball with one frozen cheese ball. Refrigerate.

Remove the pork chops from the brine, discarding the brine. Pat dry with paper towels.

Using a sharp knife, butterfly cut each pork chop. You will need to make an incision about 4 in/10 cm along the meaty side of each pork chop. Try to keep your cut in the middle of the meat so that both sides of the cut chop are equal in thickness.

Place one cheese-stuffed meat-a-ball on a baking sheet. Splay a pork chop open and place it over the top of the meat-a-ball, with the bone sticking up, sort of like a Mohawk haircut, and the meat on either side of the meat-a-ball. Gently press the chop around the meat-a-ball. Repeat with remaining meat-a-balls and chops. Refrigerate for 1 hour.

Place the planks in a pan with enough water to cover them, and top with a plate or some other weight to keep them submerged for about 1 hour.

Brush the pork chops with olive oil and season with salt and pepper.

Prepare an outdoor grill to cook direct at medium-high. Drain the planks and place them on the grill; heat until you hear the first crackle and see whiffs of smoke coming from the planks, 5 or 6 minutes. Flip them over and remove from the grill. Change the grill to cook indirect over medium heat. Place the planks back on the grill, charred-side facing up; this will allow them to flatten so that they don't curl when cooking. Place three pork chop–meatball bundles on each plank, evenly spaced with the bone sticking up as before. Close the lid and cook for 20 to 30 minutes, until the cheese starts to ooze and the chops have reached an internal temperature of 150°F/65°C. Transfer the chops to a platter. Let them rest for 5 minutes, covered loosely with a sheet of aluminum foil, before serving.

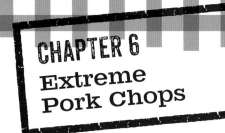

CHAPTER 6
Extreme Pork Chops

Not all pork chops are cooked by your grandma. Some of us like to cook things that are a little different, and that's what "extreme" pork chops are all about. This is where I've put all of my crazy out-of-the-box ideas for cooking pork chops. These ideas come from many places. When I see a deep-fryer out in the yard on Thanksgiving, I think it would be a good way to cook big thick pork chops. When I eat pastrami at the deli, I think it would be a good way to treat a pork chop. And when I eat French toast, I wonder how much better it would be if it had a pork chop stuffed in the middle. Yep, that's how my brain works and how much I love pork chops! And just in case my creations weren't enough, I asked my sister Doenee to do an extreme pork chop recipe and she delivered in a big way. So when you're feeling frisky and the same ol' pork chop recipe just isn't going to satisfy you, this is the place to look. Have some fun with these, because I sure did when I was making them up.

PORK CHOP–STUFFED FRENCH TOAST

French toast stuffing usually involves something sweet and creamy—like another topping, but stuffed in the middle. In my world, though, you stuff the French toast with a pork chop and it really turns it into something special. I use store-bought Texas toast and thinly slice it to open like a book and that works well, but if you've got some homemade bread, I think it'll be even better. Just slice it thick and follow the recipe.

½ tsp salt

½ tsp sugar

¼ tsp black pepper

¼ tsp cinnamon

6 boneless pork chops, about ¼ in/3 cm thick

6 eggs

¼ cup/60 ml milk

½ tsp vanilla extract

6 thick slices white bread, Texas toast style

4 tbsp/55 g butter

Preheat the broiler on high, with the rack 5 to 6 in/ 12 to 15 cm from the heat. In a small bowl, mix together the salt, sugar, pepper, and cinnamon. Season the pork chops on both sides with the salt mixture. Place the chops on a baking sheet and broil for 2 to 3 minutes, until lightly browned. Flip the chops and cook for 2 to 3 minutes more, until firm to the touch. Transfer the chops to a plate. Tent loosely with aluminum foil and set aside.

In a shallow bowl, whisk together the eggs, milk, and vanilla until frothy. With a sharp serrated knife, split the bread horizontally, leaving one end intact like a book. Place a pork chop inside each slice of bread. Preheat a large skillet over medium-low heat. Add 2 tbsp of the butter and heat until melted. Dip one bread package into the egg mixture, coating well. Place it directly in the skillet. Repeat for two more slices, or whatever will fit in your pan. Cook for 2 to 3 minutes, until golden brown. Flip and cook 2 to 3 minutes more, until the other side is golden brown. Transfer the stuffed toast to a platter and cover loosely. Repeat the process, using the remaining butter and bread until done. Serve immediately.

DOENEE'S HAWAIIAN PORK CHOP SANDWICHES

This recipe comes from my sister Denise, also known in the family as Doenee. It was her idea all the way, even though she lives in Wisconsin and has never been to Hawaii. Maybe someday she will be able to go, but for now she's doing very well with the native flavors and those cute little Hawaiian buns. Add creamy potato salad on the side and you've got a little bit of paradise on a plate.

MARINADE

¾ cup/180 ml soy sauce

¼ cup/60 ml apple cider vinegar

¼ cup/50 g packed brown sugar

2 garlic cloves, minced

1 tbsp cornstarch

1 tsp granulated sugar

½ tsp black pepper

6 boneless pork chops, about ¾ in/2 cm thick

2 tbsp vegetable oil

2 yellow onions, sliced into thin rings

SAUCE

1 cup/240 ml plain Greek yogurt

One 8-oz/225-g can crushed pineapple, well drained

2 scallions, thinly sliced

¼ tsp black pepper

6 sweet hamburger buns (such as King's Hawaiian)

TO MAKE THE MARINADE: Add the soy sauce, vinegar, brown sugar, garlic, cornstarch, granulated sugar, pepper, and 1 tbsp water to a medium saucepan over medium heat. Bring to a simmer and cook for 2 to 3 minutes, stirring often, until heated through. Transfer it to a bowl and refrigerate for at least 2 hours, until cold.

Reserve ¼ cup/60 ml of the marinade to be used later. Pierce the pork chops on both sides with a fork. Place the chops in a large zip-top bag. Pour the remaining marinade over the chops and seal, pressing out as much air as possible. Refrigerate for at least 8 hours and up to 12.

Heat the vegetable oil in a large skillet over medium heat. Add the onions and cook for 20 to 25 minutes, tossing occasionally, until golden brown and caramelized. Remove from the heat and set aside.

TO MAKE THE SAUCE: Add the yogurt, pineapple, scallions, and pepper to a medium bowl. Mix well. Cover and set aside.

Preheat the broiler on high, with the rack about 8 in/ 20 cm from the heat. Remove the chops from the marinade and pat them dry with a paper towel. Discard the used marinade. Place the chops on a baking sheet and broil for 8 to 10 minutes, until golden brown. Flip and cook for 6 to 8 minutes more, until golden brown and cooked to an internal temperature of 150°F/65°C. Transfer the chops to a platter to rest for 5 minutes.

To serve, place a chop on each of the buns. Brush with the reserved marinade. Top with some of the caramelized onions. Spread the yogurt sauce on each bun top, dividing it evenly, and place on top of the sandwiches.

BUFFALO HOT CHOP SANDWICHES

SERVES 4

Here is another classic combination of flavors that's coming over to the pork side. This sandwich is leaner and more healthful than the original deep-fried wings and much less of a mess to eat. The spicy hot sauce, blue cheese, and celery hold up that classic flavor, but for a big bonus it tastes like a pork chop. Homemade onion rings might require some extra effort, but I can't even begin to tell you how great they are with this sandwich.

½ cup/75 g crumbled blue cheese

½ cup/70 g finely chopped celery

¼ cup/55 g mayonnaise

2 tbsp vegetable oil

¼ cup/35 g all-purpose flour

½ tsp salt

½ tsp black pepper

½ tsp paprika

4 boneless pork chops, about ½ in/12 mm thick

¼ cup/55 g butter, melted

½ cup/120 ml Frank's Red Hot Sauce

4 large round buns

Preheat the broiler on high. In a medium bowl, combine the blue cheese, celery, and mayonnaise. Mix well and set aside.

Heat the oil in a large skillet over medium heat. On a flat plate, mix together the flour, salt, pepper, and paprika. Dredge the chops in the flour mixture, coating well on all sides. Shake off any excess. Place the chops in the skillet and cook for about 4 minutes, until golden brown. Flip and cook for about 4 minutes more, until golden brown and cooked to an internal temperature of 150°F/65°C. Transfer them to a plate lined with paper towels to drain.

In a medium, flat, microwave-safe bowl, whisk together the butter and hot sauce. Microwave on high for 15 seconds to warm.

Toast the buns on the cut sides under the broiler until golden brown. Dunk each chop in the hot sauce mixture, shaking off any excess. Place it on a bun bottom. Top with one-fourth of the blue cheese mixture and the top of the bun before serving.

PHILLY CHEESE CHOPS

SERVES 4

The classic Philly cheese sandwich gets a real extreme modification for this dish. The folks in Philly may have to reconsider the original after they try my pork chop version! Get some good crusty bread and don't skimp on the Cheez Whiz. Those are the key ingredients and even I wouldn't change them. I make some pretty good potato chips at home and they go well with this sandwich.

6 boneless pork chops, about ¼ in/6 mm thick

Salt

Black pepper

Paprika

½ cup/130 g Cheez Whiz

4 tbsp/60 ml vegetable oil

1 yellow onion, halved and very thinly sliced

Two 8-in/20-cm hoagie rolls, split

Season the chops well on both sides with salt, pepper, and paprika and set aside. Put the Cheez Whiz in a microwave-safe bowl and set aside. Heat 2 tbsp of the vegetable oil in a large skillet over medium heat. Add the onion, breaking up all the rings. Cook the onion, stirring occasionally, until it is very soft but not browned, 8 to 10 minutes. Transfer the onion to a bowl and set aside.

Add the remaining 2 tbsp oil to the skillet and raise the heat to medium-high. Add the pork chops and cook for 3 to 4 minutes, until golden brown. Flip and cook another 3 to 4 minutes, until the chops are browned and firm to the touch. Transfer the chops directly to the hoagie buns, shingling three on each bun. Top each sandwich with half of the onion. Microwave the Cheez Whiz until just melted. Top each sandwich with half of it and spread evenly. Cut the sandwiches in half to serve.

PIG WINGS WITH SPICY MUSTARD DIPPING SAUCE

The only thing that could make wings better is to make them out of pork chops, so that's what we're doing here. Just buy thick boneless chops and cut each one into long strips that look like boneless wings. Grill them up and make my spicy mustard dipping sauce and everybody is going to be happy. I serve these simply with cheese and crackers on the side.

4 boneless pork chops, 1¼ in/3 cm thick

1 tbsp paprika

1 tsp salt

1 tsp black pepper

1 tsp granulated garlic

1 tsp granulated onion

1 tsp Sugar In The Raw

SAUCE

¼ cup/60 g yellow mustard

¼ cup/60 g Dijon mustard

¼ cup/85 g honey

1 tbsp hot sauce

1 tbsp horseradish

½ tsp wasabi paste

Prepare an outdoor grill to cook direct over medium-high heat. Cut each pork chop into three long, even strips. In a small bowl, combine the paprika, salt, pepper, granulated garlic, granulated onion, and sugar. Mix well. Season the "wings" liberally with the spice blend and set aside.

TO MAKE THE SAUCE: In a medium bowl, combine the two mustards, honey, hot sauce, horseradish, and wasabi paste. Mix well and set aside.

Grill the pork chop strips, turning often, for 6 to 7 minutes, until the pork is golden brown and cooked to an internal temperature of 150°F/65°C. Transfer the strips to a platter to serve with the spicy mustard sauce for dipping.

PASTRAMI PORK CHOPS

This is a fun way to prepare pork chops with that distinct pastrami taste. As with any cured meat, the flavor is rich and intense, so it's not really a chop to be eaten whole. I like to slice them thinly and use the slices in a creative fashion. Some things I've tried are adding this version to a meat and cheese tray, using it for a Reuben sandwich, on top of a cheeseburger, or in a pork chop pastrami omelet.

DRY CURE

⅓ cup/75 g Morton's Tender Quick

⅓ cup/65 g packed brown sugar

2 tbsp garlic powder

2 tbsp ground coriander

6 boneless pork chops, about 1 in/2.5 cm thick

DRY RUB

1 tbsp black pepper

1½ tsp ground coriander

TO MAKE THE DRY CURE: In a shallow bowl, combine the Tender Quick, brown sugar, garlic powder, and coriander.

Press a chop down into the dry cure, coating it as heavily as possible on all sides. Transfer the chop to a large zip-top bag. Repeat with the other chops. Pour any remaining dry cure over the chops. Press as much air out of the bag as possible and then seal it. Refrigerate for 2 days, occasionally rubbing the mixture into the chops through the bag.

Prepare an outdoor grill to cook direct over medium-high heat, using apple wood for smoke flavor if desired. Rinse the chops thoroughly under cold running water and then pat them dry.

TO MAKE THE DRY RUB: Combine the pepper and coriander in a small bowl. Mix well.

Season the chops with the dry rub. Place them directly on the grill and cook for about 5 minutes, until golden brown. Flip the chops and cook another 5 minutes, until they reach an internal temperature of 150°F/65°C. Transfer the chops to a plate and tent loosely with aluminum foil. Let rest for 5 minutes or cool completely. Slice thinly on the diagonal to serve.

HORSERADISH-CRUSTED PORK CHOPS

SERVES 4

Creating an extreme dish using horseradish is pretty simple. As a matter of fact, it would be hard to create a dish with horseradish that *wasn't* considered extreme. In this case, the Parmesan cheese mellows out the spiciness of the horseradish and the bacon gives it a nice kick so it all comes together on the pork chop. A well-rounded meal in my house might include scalloped potatoes and a green vegetable.

4 boneless pork chops, about 1 in/2.5 cm thick

Salt

Black pepper

¼ cup/60 g prepared horseradish

¼ cup/30 g finely grated Parmesan cheese

¼ cup/30 g dry bread crumbs

2 slices bacon, cooked and finely chopped

1 tsp minced fresh parsley

Preheat the broiler on high, with the rack about 8 in/20 cm from the heat. Season the pork chops on both sides with salt and pepper. In a small bowl, combine the horseradish, Parmesan, bread crumbs, bacon, parsley, ¼ tsp salt, and ¼ tsp pepper. Mix well using a fork.

Place the chops on a baking sheet and broil for 6 to 8 minutes, until golden brown. Flip and cook them for 6 to 8 minutes more, until golden brown and cooked to an internal temperature of 150°F/65°C. Flip the chops and top each with one-fourth of the horseradish mixture, spreading it evenly across the top of the chop. Return to the broiler and cook for 2 to 3 minutes, until the topping is golden brown. Transfer the chops to a platter to rest for 5 minutes, then serve.

GRILLED COFFEE-CRUSTED PORK CHOPS

I like to use coffee in grilling rubs because it adds an earthy flavor unlike anything else. It's a strong ingredient, but when it's paired with salt and sugar, the flavor is quite good on pork. If possible, I get the coffee ground finely, but it's really not necessary. As the meat cooks, the coffee grounds hydrate and become soft and part of the crust. Cheesy double-baked potatoes contrast nicely with the sweetness of these chops.

1 tbsp ground coffee

1½ tsp salt

1½ tsp Sugar In The Raw

¼ tsp cayenne pepper

¼ tsp granulated onion

¼ tsp granulated garlic

¼ tsp ground cinnamon

6 bone-in pork chops, about ¾ in/2 cm thick

Prepare an outdoor grill to cook direct over medium heat. In a small bowl, combine the coffee, salt, sugar, cayenne, granulated onion, granulated garlic, and cinnamon. Mix well. Season the pork chops on both sides, dividing the seasoning evenly and using it all. Place the chops on the cooking grate and cook for 4 to 5 minutes, until deep brown. Flip the chops and cook for 4 to 5 minutes more, until deep brown and cooked to an internal temperature of 150°F/65°C. Transfer to a platter to let rest for 5 minutes, then serve.

DEEP-FRIED PORK CHOPS

SERVES 4

This is definitely one of my more extreme ideas for pork chops, but it works great. When they're done, the chops are deep brown and crusty on the outside and tender, pink, and juicy on the inside. The recipe calls for doing one or two at a time in the kitchen, but this is a great opportunity to cook a lot of chops for a party using an outdoor fryer. Amp up the indulgence factor with macaroni and cheese on the side.

1 tbsp salt

1 tbsp granulated garlic

1 tbsp granulated onion

1 tbsp chili powder

½ tsp cayenne pepper

4 bone-in porterhouse pork chops, 1¼ in/3 cm thick

Vegetable oil

In a small bowl, mix together the salt, granulated garlic, granulated onion, chili powder, and cayenne. Season the chops liberally on all sides with the seasoning mix.

In a deep 4- to 6-qt/3.8- to 5.7-L saucepan (or deep fryer), add enough vegetable oil to bring it to a depth of 3 in/7.5 cm. Over medium-high heat and using a thermometer, bring the oil to 350°F/180°C. Drop one chop into the oil and adjust the heat to maintain the temperature. If your pot is big enough to fit them comfortably, you can do two chops at a time. Cook for 8 minutes, until the chop is deep brown. With long tongs, remove the chop from the oil and drain it on a paper towel. When the oil is back to 350°F/180°C, drop in another chop and repeat the process until all the chops have been cooked. Let the chops rest for 5 minutes before serving.

JALAPEÑO PORK CHOPS

It's no surprise that pork chops and jalapeños go together well. The sweet pork combined with the spicy pepper is a natural, but any dish with three large jalapeños qualifies as extreme to me. For this extreme but simple dish, I sauté it all in a skillet and finish with the jalapeño mixture topping the chops. If you are a fire eater, leave the seeds in and add another jalapeño. Serve with mashed potatoes.

¼ cup/30 g all-purpose flour

½ tsp chili powder

¾ tsp salt

¾ tsp black pepper

3 tbsp vegetable oil

4 bone-in pork chops, about ¾ in/2 cm thick

3 large jalapeños, seeded and finely chopped

6 to 8 scallions, white and firm green parts sliced

2 large Roma tomatoes, seeded and finely chopped

2 garlic cloves, crushed

On a flat plate, mix together the flour, chili powder, ½ tsp of the salt, and ½ tsp of the pepper. Heat 2 tbsp of the vegetable oil in a large skillet over medium-high heat. Dredge the chops in the flour mixture, coating well on all sides. Shake off any excess. Place the chops in the skillet and cook for 4 to 5 minutes, until golden brown.

In a medium bowl, combine the jalapeños, scallions, tomatoes, garlic, and the remaining 1 tbsp oil, ¼ tsp salt, and ¼ tsp pepper. Flip the chops and cook for 2 minutes more. Top the chops with the jalapeño mixture, spreading it evenly. Cover the skillet and cook for 2 minutes. Flip the chops, placing them on top of the jalapeño mixture. Cover and cook for 3 to 4 minutes, until liquid forms in the bottom of the skillet. Flip the chops again. Cover and cook 3 to 4 minutes more, until the liquid has mostly evaporated. Transfer the chops to a platter and top with the jalapeño mixture. Let them rest for 5 minutes before serving.

INDEX